D1635569

Samuel Johnson

Learning Resource Services: Coleg Powys

000618

Samuel Johnson

Timothy Wilson Smith

HAUS PUBLISHING • LONDON

COLEG POWYS
BRECON

First published in Great Britain in 2004 by
Haus Publishing Limited
26 Cadogan Court, Draycott Avenue
London SW3 3BX

Copyright ©Timothy Wilson Smith, 2004

The moral right of the authors has been asserted

A CIP catalogue record for this book is available from the British Library

ISBN 1-904341-81-0

Designed and typeset in Garamond by Falcon Oast Graphic Art
Printed and bound by Graphicom in Vicenza, Italy

Front cover: Courtesy Topham Picturepoint

CONDITIONS OF SALE
All rights reserved. No part of this publication may be reproduced, stored in a
retrieval system, or transmitted in any form or by any means, electronic,
mechanical, photocopying, recording or otherwise, without the prior permission
of the publisher

This book is sold subject to the condition that it shall not, by way of trade
or otherwise, be lent, re-sold, hired out or otherwise circulated without
the publisher's prior consent in any form of binding or cover other than
that in which it is published and without a similar condition including
this condition being imposed on the subsequent purchaser

Contents

Introduction

The reason why most people want to know about Samuel Johnson (1709–84) is that they have heard of him through his biographers. The most obvious subjects for biographies are kings and queens, soldiers and sailors. Others – explorers and social reformers, artists and poets – are regarded as attractive because of the nobility or extravagance of their lives. But Johnson, though admired as a writer, has been remembered above all as a talker. Even while he was alive, acquaintances and friends wanted to let the world know that they had gained their knowledge of him by knowing him well. Among these claimants, Sir John Hawkins (1719–89) an expert on the history of music, laid claim to him because he could look back to the 1740s for his earliest memories of Johnson. However, two others had just cause to say they knew him better.

In the 1760s, Hester Thrale (1741–1821), wife of a wealthy brewer, befriended Johnson when he was near to despair. She kept him as a member of her households until her first husband died, only to eject him when she married her children's singing master. Her memoir was an act of self-justification.

At much the same time, James Boswell (1740–1795), the heir to a Scots title, made himself a friend of Johnson's in much the same way as he made himself known to Rousseau, Voltaire and David Hume. Like Zelig, Woody Allen's anti-hero, who managed to have himself photographed alongside the great and the good, Boswell had an ability to collect the famous. Still, his *Life of Johnson* put to flight all of its rivals.

Johnson was treated so much as the oracle of good taste and good sense that the Romantics and the Victorians tended to rebel against his literary, moral and political views. Twentieth-century writers rediscovered a man who was much less sure of himself than the 19th-century critics had imagined: his good sense was not easily acquired; he was more emotional than he liked to appear; and his voice was less pompous than many had decided.

Among academic experts, James L Clifford undiscovered the early life of a sympathetic Johnson, John Wain had the advantage of being a poet too, and Walter Jackson Bate brought the resources of decades of Anglo-American scholarship to the task of recreating a magisterial view of a grand, if flawed figure.

Others have been more intrigued by the stories about himself that Boswell did not tell Johnson or, perhaps that Boswell had suppressed. The popular historian Christopher Hibbert has drawn attention to the strange group of misfits for whom Johnson had provided a home. More recently, Richard Holmes, the most eminent of Romantic biographers, has focussed on Johnson's unlikely friendship with Richard Savage (1697/8–1743), a man who cast himself in the role of rejected poet, a role nobody was meant to play for at least another 50 years. Beryl Bainbridge, the historical novelist has tried to recreate his life with the Thrales. Quite simply, such a man can be approached from many directions.

The simplest way is from the beginning, before he was Johnson to his friends, let alone Doctor Johnson to the world, when he was Samuel or Sam to his family.

A young provincial scholar • 1709–37

On Wednesday, 18 September 1709 in a handsome house in the main square of Lichfield, cathedral city of Staffordshire, 40-year-old Sarah Johnson gave birth to her first-born son, Samuel. The birth was long and difficult and Mrs Johnson was assisted by a male midwife who lived just a hundred yards away.

Johnson would later write: *I was born almost dead and could not cry for some time.*[1] His parents were so worried that he might not live long that he was baptised in his mother's bedroom only hours after his birth. His father Michael, who had just been named Sheriff of the town, insisted that his child should be treated in a way that was normal for the children of families of some status. Thus, baby Sam was quickly consigned to the care of a wet-nurse. It was a decision that would cause him health problems for life, for the son of Johnson's nurse had the tubercular illness known as scrofula, a condition that affected the lymph glands. Sam contracted the disease from his nurse, which left his face marked and his eyesight poor – he was virtually blind in one eye – and his worried parents decided on an ancient remedy.

In 1712, Sam's mother took him to London to have the child 'touched' by Queen Anne at a ceremony in St James's Palace. The royal touch, believed to convey miraculous powers of healing, failed to heal him and Sam remained sickly all his life. In later years, he would claim to remember a lady in a black hood and thought he had heard another baby crying in another part of the building. The occasion was his first visit to the city that would be his home almost all his adult life. He received a memento of the trip: a gold coin given to him by the Queen that he wore round his neck for the rest of his life.

Sam was prone to physical affliction: he would later survive an attack of smallpox and in early adulthood he developed nervous ticks that made a grotesque young man look like an idiot. It is possible that he suffered from Tourette's syndrome. He was always strange but his ability to surmount illness marked him out as a survivor. He became large and strong, an ugly eccentric who would never be missed in a crowd.

Lichfield was in the heart of England. Its founding patron was St Chad. In the 7th century Theodore of Tarsus, the only Greek Archbishop of Canterbury, consecrated Chad, a monk from the Anglian kingdom of Northumbria, as first bishop of the diocese of the Middle Anglians or Mercians, whose kingdom occupied approximately the area covered by the modern English midlands. A century later, Chad's name was given to a beautiful manuscript of the Gospels illuminated in the cathedral library. By then, Chad's shrine was the centre of a cult, and round it was built a succession of cathedrals, the last of which, the present building, is topped by three elegant spires. From its origins, Lichfield was a place known for piety and learning and, as in many county towns in the Midlands – another example is Stratford – its special character was preserved after the Reformation by its grammar school.

Lichfield suited a boy who came from a devout and bookish background. Provincial it may have been, but it was neither inward looking nor complacent. Johnson was proud of his hometown and would retain traces of his Staffordshire accent all his life. Thus, he pronounced the drink punch as 'poonsh'.

By tradition, Lichfield was a royalist town and had endured the blows of defeat during the civil war. Loyalty to the Crown came to mean much to young Samuel. A boy from the neighbourhood of Lichfield had been registered as cured by Charles II of 'the King's evil', the popular name for scrofula and in 1687, James II (1685–88) had come to the cathedral to 'touch' anyone suffering from scrufola.

Johnson's relatively elderly parents were ill at ease with children. His father had a good reason for being away from home. As a bookseller, Michael Johnson had to go on his travels, for in that age his profession involved him in deals far from home. The large house that he had built at the corner of the

The Johnson home on the market square in Lichfield

market square – in which his children were born – was a sign of his aspirations rather than his prosperity. He did not need 15 rooms for living space and for storage, but a splendid home that was also a business base may have been the response of a poor man who was habituated to the persistent references of an ignorant wife to her genteel connections. He was not even a good businessman – he got into debt early on and as he grew older the deficit mounted.

Anxiety about money plagued the Johnson household: Michael's idea of economy was to ask his wife to cut down on her social visits; Sarah's was to ask him to be more careful with his accounts; and neither was able to fulfil the task set by the other. In his books, Michael found a refuge from uncomfortable truths; his wife gave him no intellectual companionship and he was not around to know the son who had inherited his mental gifts.

Despite the signs of tension between the two of them, Sam thought his parents had a good marriage, at least in so far *as they did not live ill together*.[2] *I did not respect my mother*, he said later, *though I loved her*.[3] She indulged his whims, among them his desire for little luxuries such as coffee, while insisting on strict standards of behaviour. When Sam's brother Nathaniel (Nat) was born in 1712, the two naturally developed sibling jealousy and Sam thought his mother lacked the skill to act as a just judge in their childish disputes.

Sam did not treat Nat kindly and, while he eventually left Lichfield, his brother lived at home to work in the bookshop until his sudden death at the age of 24. Sam never wrote or spoke much about him, but his affection for his mother never wavered. When he married, he chose a wife who was closer to his mother's age than to his own and, when he learnt that his mother was dying, he made great efforts to get home from London. By contrast, he had completely ignored his brother's death.

As a child, Johnson showed signs of exceptional intelligence, which Michael loved to indicate to the neighbours. His mother taught him to spell 'Natty' at the time of his brother's baptism. At the age of four, he composed four funny lines about the death of a duck on which he had trodden, but he told Boswell that the author of part of the verse was his father. He blamed his father for drawing attention to him and, if he thought there would be company in the house, he would run away and hide in a tree. Johnson retained a lifelong hatred of demonstrations of precocity. When a friend wished him to judge which of his two sons recited Gray's *Elegy* with more skill, he suggested that they should say it simultaneously, to make more noise and finish the noise more quickly. The remark may have sounded cruel but the emotional force behind it came from painful experience that *the life of an old man's child* is like that of *a little boy's dog*.[4] He loathed being anyone's toy.

When Sam was about four, he went to the infant school run by

Dame Alice Oliver. He recalled her with affection and she thought of him as 'the best scholar she ever had'.⁵ Two years later he progressed to a school for older children run by one Thomas Browne, who was rash enough to dedicate a book he had written on spelling to the universe. The universe, alas, did not read it.

Of his early education, Johnson could not recall much other than the occasion when he first heard the tale of St George and the dragon. *Babies,* he told Mrs Thrale, *do not long to know about other babies like Goody Two Shoes. They want to be told about fairies and castles.*⁶ When she pointed out that stories about good babies sold well, he retorted that parents buy books that their children chose not to read.

At the age of seven and a half, his education became serious when he joined the lower school of Lichfield Grammar School. The curriculum and style of teaching at such institutions had been set in the 16th century at St Paul's, London, which had been founded by Dean Colet, mentor of Thomas More, and whose first High Master had been William Lily. Lily's *Grammar* was the standard textbook until it was supplanted in the 19th century by Kennedy's *Latin Primer*. What Lily inculcated was the systematic understanding of a dead language. Lessons involved endless repetition and thorough drills. Schooling was not meant to be fun or in any obvious sense useful. Useful learning was available in nonconformist academies which prepared their pupils for a trade.

The Church of England,

In the 18th century, the word 'literate' meant a person who could read and write Latin. Medieval Latin was largely an idiom of the Church while classical Latin, spoken by the cleverest men, was wholly the product of a pagan civilisation. As most schoolmasters were clerics, this could create problems of taste and conscience. But the lure of decadent morals was not felt by those who struggled to read and repeat the rules set out by Lily and those later pedagogues who had supplemented and revised his text.

which outside the colleges of Oxford, Cambridge, Winchester and Eton chose to worship God only in English, prepared its clergy to teach the faithful by making them Latinists.

Such schooling emphasised the importance of memory and, although at first Johnson struggled to cope with the quantity of information he had to absorb, he soon found that he had an unusual ability to retain it. He became used to excelling his contemporaries in weekly tests and they learned to accept his intellectual dominance. This compensated for his physical disabilities – probably, he could not catch a ball – but it did not make him a wimp. Johnson enjoyed jumping, tree climbing and swimming at a time when few people could swim – and he could hold his own in any fight. He made one good friend, Edmund Hector (1708–94) whose uncle had assisted at his birth, and he was 'indulged and caressed'[7] by the schoolmaster, Sir Humphrey Hawkins, who taught him with love.

At the age of nine, Johnson moved to the Upper School where he was taught by Mr Holbrooke, a boring young pedant, and by Mr Hunter, the headmaster who had a reputation as a flogger. As an adult, Sam did not object to corporal punishment, only to the way it was given. *My master whipped me very well. Without that I should have done nothing.*[8] But of Hunter he said: *He was not severe, Sir. A master ought to be severe. Sir, he was cruel.*[9] Other pupils spoke of Hunter's learning and his love of music, but Johnson always remembered him with fear.

Details of Johnson's school work are not recorded, yet it can be assumed that he worked his way through the myths recounted by Ovid, legends found in Virgil, history retailed by Livy and Caesar, the orations of Cicero. He would have studied enough Greek to read the New Testament and some poetry, but the lyrics he enjoyed were by Horace and the satires he admired were those of Juvenal. Like most grammar school boys, he was more familiar with Latin than with Greek; unlike most he wrote Latin prose and verse with ease.

Such an education served any number of European men well for 500 years. However, it did not prepare them for an obvious career, except in the case of those who wished to pass it on: from the pulpit, in a lecture hall, in a class room, in a coffee house, in a gentleman's club or from the printing press. Johnson had a vocation to educate but he had not found a way to express it. He might become a learned bookseller in the wake of his father or follow Hawkins's example by becoming a little regarded, much loved usher in charge of young boys.

Decisions were taken out of his hands by the arrival in Lichfield of Cornelius Ford (1694–1731), a young don at Peterhouse, Cambridge and Sam's cousin on his mother's side. Ford had come to put the Johnson family affairs in order: Michael owed four years of back taxes to the Commissioners of Excise that he could not pay. Ford settled the debt, put the house into a family trust and was struck by the brilliant boy who lived there. The don offered to take Sam home with him. Sam was delighted that he would miss school; he was in a state of adolescent rebellion and refused to go to church. Ford, he was sure, would understand him better than his parents did.

Ford was a man of the world who loved learning but thought a purely academic life tedious. Now married to a conveniently well-to-do wife, he had had to resign his fellowship and like any ex-don he had taken a country parish as his home. However, he had no intention of being bound by his duties there. A bright, ungainly cousin would be an interesting distraction. Ford was agreeable, sophisticated and kind. Johnson had never met anyone like him.

Ford invited him to visit the rectory near Stourbridge and he ended up staying there for nine months. Mrs Thrale said that Johnson spoke of Cornelius Ford 'always with tenderness, praising his acquaintance with life and manners'.[10] Johnson had found a person smarter than his schoolmasters, with a wider knowledge of the classics, who spoke with assurance about modern writers from the restoration of King Charles II in 1660 to the death of Queen Anne in 1714. But he was not just widely read in modern works. He also impressed Sam with his knowledge of modern ways or 'manners' and, therefore, of how modern people lived. Given the choice between authority and experience, Johnson chose the latter. In this, he would show himself the disciple of Cornelius Ford.

Johnson's earliest writings from the Stourbridge period of his life are of interest only to scholars except in so far as they show that he was already keen to be a writer. Writers, however, had to be educated and he had not yet finished his studies in Lichfield. He wanted to go back to the grammar school but because of his long absence without leave, Mr Hunter would not have him back. It was probably Ford who used his influence to find Johnson a place in the grammar school at Stourbridge.

There, too, Johnson seems to have annoyed the headmaster, for when he heard that the post of usher was available he applied for it and was turned down. An usher may have been on the lowliest rung in the teaching profession, as he did not need a university degree and he was always badly paid, but it was better to be poor than to have nothing. The alternative was to work in the family bookshop.

Johnson would have been in despair if he had not come across another worldly cleric to boost his sense of worth: Gilbert Walmesley (1680–1751). Walmesley was a comfortable bachelor in his late 40s, a church lawyer who leased the Bishop's Palace while the bishop lived elsewhere, and who enjoyed the company of bright young men at his well-stocked table.

At Walmseley's, Johnson met an amusing child actor. In adult life, David Garrick (1717–79), son of an army captain whose Huguenot parents had fled from persecution in France, would be one of his favourite sparring partners. However, at the time, the boy may have seemed merely diverting, for Johnson's attention was focused on Walmesley himself.

Years later, Johnson summed up his own contradictory feelings about his mentor. *He was a Whig, with all the virulence and malevolence of his party; yet difference of opinion did not keep us apart. I honoured him and he endured me.*[11] Their relationship was based on its lack of ease as each found the views of the other repellent. Each admired the other's ability to defend those repellent views. The experience taught Johnson that arguing for a cause was one of his special talents but also that an even more precious gift was his flair for friendship.

It also highlighted another problem: Whigs such as Walmesley held the commanding heights in both state and church. So, how could Johnson, a Tory like his father, achieve the success for which he longed? Tories tended to be obscure country squires or parson; aristocrats and bishops were Whigs.

There was one famous institution that since the civil war in the previous century had been the home of lost causes: the University of Oxford. Early in 1728, Sarah Johnson inherited a legacy of £40 for her 'own separate use'[12], and a wealthy school friend, Andrew Corbet, who had gone to Pembroke College, offered to meet some of Johnson's expenses if he would come there. There were family connections with that College and in late October, Sam and Michael set out for Oxford, where Sam was received into Pembroke College.

Young Sam was soon in trouble for avoiding classes that did not excite him or leaving exercises incomplete if he judged them pointless. He did not escape routine punishments, but his tutor decided it was a better idea to set him a task that would stretch him. He told him to translate into Latin a work by the leading poet of the day: 'Messiah' by Alexander Pope. It was a resounding success and via a third party, probably the son of Pope's close friend Dr Arbuthnot, Sam's verses reached the great man himself.

After the restoration of the monarchy in 1660, John Dryden (1631–1700) became the leading English man of letters. Playwright, literary critic and poet, he was valued above all for his verse satires, such as 'Absolom and Achitophel' and 'Macflecknoe', which were largely written in rhyming couplets

The form was later perfected by Alexander Pope (1688–1744). Pope's output was more restricted than Dryden's – he did not match his achievements as a playwright or as a writer of prose – but he was more versatile in the use of his medium and had a wider range of satirical targets, as in the different targets of 'The Rape of the Lock' and 'The Epistle to Burlington'

Pope said, 'The writer of this poem will leave it a question for posterity, whether his or mine be the original.'[13] For pleasure, Johnson also translated bits of John Dryden, the great poet of the late-17th century.

Dryden and Pope became Johnson's poetic models – both were translators themselves as well as masters of satire and Dryden was a dramatist and an essayist, too.

Like them, Johnson aspired to be a man of letters. He may have noticed that they chose to be or were outsiders, for Dryden had joined the Catholic church and Pope was brought up in it. He would have similar political views and would differ from them in just one respect: he would be loyal to the Church of England.

At Oxford, Johnson became a convinced Christian. While devoting most of his intellectual energies to improving his ancient Greek, he came upon a book by William Law, an Anglican writer who had refused to break his oath of loyalty to the Catholic King James II by accepting the Protestant Prince of Orange as King William III. Law's career had been blighted by his own exigent conscience, a trait that must have recommended him to Johnson, and he became famous as the author of *A Serious Call to a Holy Life*. Johnson read it, he told Boswell, *expecting to find it a dull book (as such books generally are), and perhaps to laugh at it. But I found Law quite an overmatch for me; and this was the first occasion of my thinking in earnest of religion, after I became capable of rational inquiry.*[14] For the rest of his life he was sure that Christianity was true, but that did not rid his mind of doubt, indeed his conviction made him painfully aware of his own failings. His conviction was intellectual, but emotionally he remained insecure.

Without a lot of work or a busy social life, Johnson was easily depressed. He considered duty all important, immorality only too attractive. He would be forever making new resolutions – he often undertook not to be lazy – and accusing himself of failing to keep them. Henceforward, religion was the rock on which his life was built. It did not make his life easy.

Oxford was not just a place for agonising about the state of his soul. Sam sought to make his mark there and was jealous that one contemporary, Jack Meeke (1709–63), was so fluent at construing the classical texts. (Meeke was eventually elected a fellow of Pembroke and on a visit many years later, Sam was delighted to see his old rival again. But he came to the conclusion that his own way outside academia had been a more fascinating route to follow.)

As a young man, Johnson was not simply a dry scholar. A school friend from his Lichfield days, John Taylor (1711–88), arrived in the spring of 1729 and told him excitedly that he was coming to Pembroke, too. Johnson advised against it – he would do better across the road at Christ Church – so to Christ Church, Taylor went. He set Taylor the task of telling him what he had just been taught there – on one particular occasion there was a hard problem in algebra to explain that Taylor forgot – and he enjoyed joining that college's set. He loved wandering in its meadows or sliding on the ice and, though he could not have seen the ball, he tried to play cricket. He grumbled about the beer.

However, the good times did not last long. The money from his mother was running out while the money promised by Andrew Corbet (1709–41) never materialised. His acquaintances noted that his shoes were falling to pieces and one young gentleman had a fresh pair left at his door. Sam threw them out. It was humiliating that Taylor's friends in the more gentlemanly college of Christ Church noticed how scruffy Sam looked.

Several months in arrears, Johnson could not pay his college bills. Near the end of 1729, he made the excuse that he had to go home for Christmas. After 13 months in his beloved Oxford, he had to leave. He hid his toes in a pair of large boots as Taylor trudged with him to Banbury. He left his books in the care of his faithful friend and went, reluctantly, back to Lichfield.

The next seven years make up a period when Johnson seemed to mark time. He tried to give a meaning to his life and he failed just as he had failed so many times before. Still, he found a wife and began on the road to London. His decision to marry affected his way of life for less than 20 years; by contrast, his decision to go to London affected the whole of the rest of his days.

Understandably, 1730 was a year when Sam moped. The route to the kind of life he wanted, as fellow of a college, was barred to him. He had thought of becoming a barrister, but the poverty that stopped him from completing his degree in letters would also prevent him from studying law. He could be an usher, for the only other course open to him was to join Michael and Natty – noisy Natty – in the bookshop.

Michael may have been near to insolvency – a venture into running a parchment factory had not worked – and it is probable that only a loan from a fellow bookstore owner in London saved Johnson senior from bankruptcy. He never repaid his friendly creditor and it was only as he was dying that Johnson would settle his father's debt with the lender's heirs. Michael never even made a will. When he died at the age of 74 in December 1731, there was little to leave his widow and sons. Natty's future was obvious – he would help his mother – but Sam had to find some means of supporting himself. He was in no state to do much.

In his mood of dejection, Sam was occasionally cheered by the usual arguments with Walmesley. He also was grateful for the attention of a young aristocrat, Cornet Henry Hervey [1701–48], son of the Earl of Bristol, who had seduced, drunk and gambled his way into the affections of people he met while stationed at Lichfield. Johnson did not delude himself about Hervey's behaviour – Hervey was the first but not the last young rake whom he found attractive – but his own awkwardness made him always susceptible to charm and he forgave in others failings he would castigate in himself. When he was impoverished in London, Johnson could call on Hervey and be sure he would be generously received. *He was a vicious man but very kind to me. If you call a dog Hervey, I shall love him.*[15]

Sam was looking to move beyond Lichfield. He managed to get the post of usher at the grammar school, Market Bosworth in Leicestershire. The statutes required the usher to be a Bachelor of Arts but the patron, Sir Wolstan Dixie (1701–67), cared nothing for rules or, indeed, for considerate behaviour. He was tyrannical and Sam was far too proud to let himself be bullied by anybody and he resigned. He applied to another school; Frewood, some 15 miles from Lichfield, but failed to get the job.

Johnson sought refuge in agreeable company. The nearest town of importance was Birmingham, only 30 miles away, and there were people he took to visiting. His old friend, Edmund Hector, was practising as a surgeon and his godfather, Dr Swinfen, was a local physician. What's more, Swinfen's daughter Elizabeth (1716–86) was married to Monsieur Desmoulins, a Huguenot refugee who was writing master at the Free Grammar School. For Dr Swinfen, Sam wrote out a description in Latin of the symptoms of his depression, which seemed pathological. Swinfen was so impressed by the lucidity of Sam's self-analysis that he broke his trust by showing the account to some acquaintances. Sam felt betrayed and never fully trusted his godfather again.

Edmund Hector was more helpful. He introduced Johnson to

A portrait of Johnson's bride Elizabeth Porter

a bookseller and would-be publisher, Thomas Warren. For Warren, Sam translated an account of the Portuguese in Abyssinia by a missionary, Father Lobo, for which he wrote a masterly preface. It was his first literary work that attracted some attention.

Hector also introduced Johnson to a draper named Harry Porter and his wife Elizabeth. The Porter family came to matter more to him, for when in 1734 Harry suddenly died, Sam's visits to the household became more frequent and gradually the widow fell in love with a young man whom she said was the most sensible man she had ever met. On 8 July 1735, Johnson, aged 25, married Elizabeth Porter (1689–1752), politely described as 40 on the marriage licence but, in fact, five years older. The marriage led to a breach between the bride and one of her sons. Only her daughter, Lucy (1715–86), became a friend of the new stepfather.

Johnson always insisted that he and 'Tetty' had married for love. The next year, with the help of his new wife's funds, Johnson set up his own school in the village of Edial, just outside Lichfield. It was intended as an establishment for the young gentlemen of Staffordshire, but most of them failed to turn up. The school was never a paying proposition and within a year it had closed.

One of the pupils would eventually be famous, for Captain Garrick enrolled his sons Peter and David. Indeed, David watched the Johnsons making love through the keyhole, or at least pretended that he had, for mocking his former teacher became a party trick of which he never tired. Master and pupil both realised that for them there was no viable future in Lichfield. Already, Johnson had contacted the leading employer of literary hacks in London, Edward Cave. From young Peter Garrick he had borrowed a book on Turkish history that gave him the idea for an exotic tragedy that might be performed only in London. Were he to go, he would have to leave his new wife behind. Meanwhile, even though David Garrick spoke of his uncle's wine business he hoped to become an actor, and that meant that he too must go to London.

On 2 March 1737, the unlikely pair set out together. Johnson left his new wife behind and rode towards the city that would become the centre of his world. While he and Garrick travelled southwards, Nathaniel Johnson took ill suddenly and died. Just days later, Captain Garrick was dead, too.

A critic comes to London • 1737–1745

Johnson had already taken to writing, but his translation of the memoirs of a Portuguese missionary to Abyssinia, Father Jerome Lobo, and the first three acts of his tragedy, *Irene*, were apprentice works that were not likely to make him famous. He was going to London in a spirit of hope, and hope sprung from desperation. The man who in maturity took on the role of tutor to the English nation was in 1737 little more than a failed teacher. He did not yet look the imposing figure familiar from the portraits of his friend Joshua Reynolds. He was bony, clumsy and strange. Those who had interviewed him for the posts he had failed to get had been worried that schoolboys, one of the most merciless tribes known to man, would have had fun at his expense.

In later years, he and Garrick used to entertain their friends with the story of how he had reached London with only two pence halfpenny in his pocket and Garrick with a penny halfpenny. Both had to find work immediately.

As a boy and young man, Johnson was often intimidated as he knew his appearance put people off: there were scars on his neck from operations on glands infected by scrofula; his face was pitted with the evidence of smallpox; he was virtually blind in his left eye and his good right eye was myopic; and in his movements, he was ungainly.

When he arrived in London, his physical disabilities had made him a marked man. Thus, friends took to warning new acquaintances that they should not be put off by his appearance or behaviour: he ate greedily, drank tea in enormous quantities and was none too clean.

Sir Joshua Reynolds' portrait of the young Samuel Johnson

In Garrick's case, this did not take long. In his father's will, he was left almost nothing because his recently deceased uncle had left him £1,000. Briefly he and his older brother were partners in the wine trade, which left him money and time enough to visit the theatre. When his mother died, he took to the stage, an unusual occupation for a gentleman, and in 1741 his efforts were rewarded when an obscure production of *Richard III* made him a star. Hogarth, with unfailing commercial sense, painted him acting the part. Garrick was famous and would soon be rich.

Unfortunately, for Johnson there was no alternative to life in a garret. The prospect did not appeal to Tetty and for a time Johnson hankered after a job as a provincial schoolmaster. However, he failed to find a job. He had to write because there was nothing else that he could do to earn money.

Perhaps his moment had come, for national politics was in a state of flux. The long rule of Sir Robert Walpole seemed

During Johnson's adolescence and early manhood, Sir Robert Walpole (1676–1745) dominated English politics. In 1721, George I had invited him to head the ministry and Walpole mastered parliament through his use of patronage and corruption.

To the country, Walpole represented stability, peace and prosperity. He was ridiculed as 'Prime Minister', then a term of abuse, but he was impervious to attack up until he lost popularity for levying the new excise tax in 1733. Walpole remained in power until 1742.

about to end, with the press leading the charge against him.

The 'prime minister' had begun to look vulnerable. The period of stability and corruption that was typical of his rule could not last for ever, his enemies believed. No longer secure at court, he was the favoured butt of caricaturists and, what was worse, the favoured target of the opposition satirists. Never before had the leading figure in English public life been attacked by such a brilliant group of men.

During the 1720s, in *Gulliver's Travels* Jonathan Swift had turned his formidable literary weapons on behaviour in modern courts, while in John Gay's *The Beggar's Opera* the criminal 'hero', Macheath the highwayman, was a thinly disguised version of Robert Walpole.

In the 1730s, Alexander Pope found an allusive way of being equally effective. Viscount Bolingbroke (1678–1751), head of Queen Anne's last Tory ministry, had been so openly opposed to the accession of George I that he had fled abroad. He came back to England after George I's death, determined to organise opposition to the government of George II. In a moment of inspiration, he opened a copy of poems by Horace and suggested to Pope that he might 'imitate' them in English. Both of them realised what points the poet could make by evoking the parallels between the England of George Augustus of Hanover and the Rome of Augustus Caesar. But while Horace had merely teased opponents, Pope savaged them. He turned a foil that touched enemies into a sabre that bludgeoned them.

Johnson took this a step further. There was one Roman satirist who was both harsher and coarser than Horace and the young Johnson knew him well. Juvenal, who belonged to Rome's silver age, had a tone that was racy, vulgar and fierce. He had been translated into English in the late-17th century by a group of writers in Dryden's set, but nobody had yet done for him what Pope had done for Horace.

In 1738, Johnson produced his first fine poem, 'London'. A skilful attempt at applying the strictures of Juvenal on ancient Rome to a modern capital city, it attracted the attention and admiration of Pope. It expressed Johnson's ambivalence about the place that came to represent all human life to him.

Johnson's need of cash, however, made any sustained assumption of a moral stance an unaffordable luxury. Pope could afford to take a lofty tone, as he was a wealthy man. The most memorable words in Johnson's work, however, which he wrote out in capital letters, *SLOW RISES WORTH, BY POVERTY DEPRESSED*,[16] come in a line that is a poignant reminder of his actual situation. His view that only a blockhead writes except for money was formed by necessity: Johnson was a hack in the pay of Edward Cave, publisher of *The Gentleman's Magazine*.

Edward Cave (1691–1754) was born near Rugby. After being expelled from the famous Rugby school, he made his way to London and in 1731, bought a small printing office in Clerkenwell. There, he began to print the *Gentleman's Magazine* whose readership eventually grew to 15,000. Cave was a striking man, over six feet tall, heavy and strong. His chief memorial was the magazine, which was still appearing 150 years after his death.

It had become difficult to attack the government. After Henry Fielding, a young playwright, had staged a drama that made fun of Walpole, the prime minister passed a law through parliament that before production the text of all future plays must be shown to the Lord Chamberlain first. Meanwhile, parliament was as touchy as its leading member. It had recently forbidden the reporting of its debates during parliamentary sessions.

The new law on the theatre turned Fielding from a master of farce into a master novelist. The new law on reporting was easier to subvert. Names could be changed, accounts of discussions could be delayed and it was easy to invent what speakers should have said.

Swift's example was contagious. In *Gulliver's Travels*, dating from a time when Walpole seemed firmly in power (1726) but had yet to ensure that he would stay in power (1727), Flimnap, the treasurer of Lilliput – in England, Walpole's title was First Lord of the Treasury – is said to perform acrobatic feats on a tight rope: 'Flimnap the Treasurer is allowed to cut a caper on the straight rope, at least an inch higher than any other lord in the whole Empire.'[17]

By the late 1730s, even Walpole, who had skilfully evaded every earlier attack on his integrity, seemed to be losing his sense of balance. His hold on the position was precarious. Corruption charges against him had never quite stuck – as Swift put it, he was marvellous at doing somersaults on the rope – but he was becoming vulnerable not so much to the attacks of the Tories as to those of rival Whigs. In 1742 he fell, a victim of the 'Patriots', who loathed the link with Hanover and who were spoiling for a fight with England's traditional foes, the French and Spaniards, both ruled by Bourbon kings.

So as to report on parliament, Johnson took from Swift the idea of Lilliput, the country of small and small-minded people, and he set his account of the debates in parliament in the Senate of Lilliput. He was not, however, a master of parody in the class of Swift. Over the years, Johnson would acquire a sure sense of the tone of other men's voices, whether a desperate clergymen pleading for pardon from the noose or the blandly assured Reynolds expounding classic art to a gathering of the great, earnestly seeking cultivation, but as yet he could not catch the vehemence of the elder Pitt or the languid superciliousness of the Earl of Chesterfield in the House of Lords. At this stage of his career, he was not versatile enough. His excursion into parliamentary reporting is of interest because what he wrote is read for pleasure. He did not like being fully committed to a career in journalism. He still wondered if he should teach, but the lack of a degree and his manner always stood in the way. A would-be helper ventured that he should apply to Swift himself, since the dean of St Patrick's Cathedral, Dublin must be influential in the same city's Trinity College. If Swift received Johnson's letter, the great man did not reply. Johnson had to accept the fact that his world was going to be the world according to Cave.

Journals had flourished in London in the 17th century and in the days of Queen Anne, *The Tatler* and *The Spectator* raised journalism to a genteel level. Cave's idea was to bring out a weekly periodical for which he invented a term: magazine. With the launch of *The Gentleman's Magazine*, Cave proved himself as the editor who first grasped that a new reading public existed. Richard Steele (1672–1729) and Joseph Addison, (1672–1719) the writers chiefly responsible for *The Tatler* and *The Spectator*, had aimed at gentlemen in the coffee houses that were a feature of modern London life. Since Cave was less polished, he fitted better into the brasher, wider world where Walpole flourished. His shrewd business sense, his awareness of the way the wind blew, his combination of loyalty and meanness to his authors were qualities that kept his team in print. Pope, who was privately kind to struggling authors, publicly disdained them. Cave, on the other hand, relied on them.

Johnson had first approached Cave from Lichfield by sending

him an arrogant letter advertising his own literary prowess. Once in London he took the trouble to meet him, the two men got on and soon each depended on the other: Johnson on Cave for a regular, if small income; Cave on Johnson for suggestions and expert advice.

Johnson offered Cave a translation of and commentary on the history of the Council of Trent by Paolo Sarpi, a Venetian cleric. In 1545–63 the Council of Trent had defined the teaching and ordered the discipline of the Catholic church. Sarpi took an extreme version of his native city's standard anti-papal attitude and, thus, he held a special fascination for a learned Protestant.

Johnson was energetic in pursuing the project and wrote several hundred pages before abandoning it in favour of easier ways of making money. He got into the habit of producing something every month. It gave him a sense of discipline that was invaluable for someone so moody. He dashed out a series of short biographies of great men – of Sarpi (a by-product of his ambitious scheme), of Herman Boerhaave (1668–1738), a celebrated Dutch physician and botanist who had died recently, of Robert Blake (1599–1657), the famous admiral of Cromwell's wars, of Sir Francis Drake (1540–96), the still more famous admiral of the Elizabethan age, and of some lesser scholars. He showed a natural sympathy for anyone involved in some form of research. He acquired habits of quickly acquiring knowledge and quickly disseminating it, and developed a number of settled views. Describing European excursions into America, he robustly attacked any sentimentality about the ways of life of the continent's natives. *The question is not, whether a good Indian or bad Englishman be most happy; but which state is most desirable, supposing virtue and reason the same.*[18] Equally characteristic was his praise of Boerhaave for his determination to succeed despite *the obstacles of poverty*[19] and because of *his insatiable curiosity of knowledge*[20] and the tough constitution that made him *insensible of* (unaware of) *any sharpness of air, or inclemency of weather.*[21]

During this period, Johnson's career gravitated around Cave's base in St John's Gate, Clerkenwell. 'London' was still effectively two cities: Westminster was home to government and political debate; London the centre of commerce and financial transactions. The link that bound the two together, as in medieval times, was still The Strand. London generated wealth, Westminster directed and appropriated it for national needs. At one time, London had been closed off at night as its gates were shut: Aldgate and Bishopsgate in the east, Newgate in the north, Ludgate in the west. Within this area lay 'the City', but 'London' had long and far outgrown it and had absorbed Westminster. It extended way down the river towards Limehouse, in the south-east as far as Deptford, in the south-west as far as Chelsea, across the river it included Southwark, in the north-west it extended to Marylebone Fields, in the north-east to Moorfields and it was bounded at the north by an outer ring road that started out as Marylebone Road and went eastwards first as Euston Road, then as Pentonville Road.

Within this large area around 1740, lived more than 600,000 people, over 10 per cent of the English population. Everyone was within easy reach of a slum, but some districts were becoming the exclusive preserves of the rich. The first attempt at creating an English equivalent to an Italian piazza was made at Covent Garden in the 17th century by the Earl of Bedford, but by 1740 that development had been claimed by its theatre and its fruit market. The fashionable area had shifted west to Mayfair, centred on the Grosvenor estate and the grandest of all squares, appropriately Grosvenor Square. Across Piccadilly there was the smart St James's Square, dating from 1720, and nearby were Leicester Fields, home to the Prince of Wales. 'Poor Fred', as he was known, was artistic and intelligent, but did not possess a forceful personality, so his presence did little to raise the tone of the place. The West End was tightly compressed. Villages such as Knightsbridge were not yet part of it and Kensington's one key feature was its royal palace, further out than the freshly built-up sites favoured by the nobility and gentry.

Since the burning down of Whitehall during the reign of William III, kings had no adequate base near the city centre. William III and Queen Anne liked Hampton Court Palace, to which Sir Christopher Wren had added modern gardens and a modern façade. While Sophia, Electress of Hanover, enjoyed the imposing Schloss of Herrenhausen, her English cousin's daughter tried to live in state in the renovated palace up the Thames, where, in Pope's words: '. . .Thou, Great Anna, whom three realms obey/ Dost sometimes Counsel take – and sometimes Tea.'[22]

Meanwhile, in Piccadilly aristocrats had built grand town houses like Devonshire House (pulled down in the 1920s) or Burlington House, and at the end of St James's Park stood Buckingham House, property of the Duke of Buckingham. Little had been done to make the Tudor St James's Palace acceptable to modern taste. Thus, in the English capital the English monarch's presence was little noticed.

What dominated the skyline were the churches. In 1750, the view along the river from Somerset House in the Strand, painted by the Venetian painter, Canaletto, showed city spires grouped round the overarching dome of St Paul's cathedral. After the Great Fire of 1666, Wren had put forward a plan to lay out a modern capital in the manner of Rome, Paris or Madrid, but the plan had been rejected in favour of maintaining the medieval maze of the London streets. Yet despite the inadequate overall scheme, Wren and his helpers and successors had created a wonderfully unified central vista that, however much London expanded in every direction, was to endure till 1940. On closer inspection, however, hidden by the noble prospect was much that was disgusting, and to harsh reality Hogarth is a more accurate guide than Canaletto. In 1731, Hogarth began to produce prints of modern moral subjects, tales of the decline and fall of unwary

William Hogarth's views of London life were often more accurate than satirical

immigrants to London, such as a girl from the country who became a harlot or a merchant's heir who turned from a rake into a madman.

Clearly, Johnson saw the squalid side of town life. If he aspired to grandeur, it was beyond his reach to attain. What was obvious to him was that he would have to struggle to survive. Tetty may have separated from Johnson temporarily, but as a wife she had little choice but to follow her husband. They moved from one set of cheap lodgings to another, in Exeter Street off The Strand, in Boswell Court, Holborn or in Bow Street. There she aged, far from her friends, and she grew fatter, dependent on alcohol and on *laudanum*, an opium product she took for pain. She resisted Sam's sexual advances and he tried to avoid being at home. He escaped to Cave's premises in St John's Gate, Clerkenwell or to a nearby tavern in Old Street. Determined to be sober, he took to drinking tea.

Meanwhile, in the man's world of 'Grub Street', the name given to the world of professional journalists, he was gradually acquiring a reputation as a reliable hack. For all his indolence, he was able to meet deadlines. But that ability made him neither satisfied nor rich. His poem *London* is a young man's protest against social injustice and political corruption: the view he expressed of his new home was defined by a mood of disillusionment. And then, quite suddenly, the place became dangerous and glamorous, for Cave introduced him to Richard Savage (1697–1743).

If other writers grumbled about their lot, Savage was a man with a mission to be a victim. He claimed to be the unwanted child of Lady Macclesfield, a society lady whose liaison with Earl Rivers led to the birth of two illegitimate children and a divorce. Even in the raffish world of late-17th century London, that made her a cause of scandal and she wisely took refuge in silence. She became simple 'Mrs Brett' and hoped for a quiet life. Savage, however, was determined not to let her have it. He wrote a poem called 'The Bastard' inscribed 'with all reverence to Mrs Brett, once Countess of Macclesfield'.[23] He terrified the old lady by arriving unannounced at her door. He told anyone who listened – and at this stage, Johnson did – about his supposed mother's unspeakable cruelties towards him, such as her plan to get rid of him in the American colonies, her manipulation of his career, her studied indifference to his fate. The only evidence for all this was always Savage's word. On his birth certificate, he was plain Richard Smith, but his godmother was the wife of Earl Rivers's agent and this was enough for him in 1715, to start calling himself 'Savage', the family name of the Rivers family – he was 17.

Savage would explain that he had been defrauded of his inheritance. He had certainly been spied upon by government informers, for his indiscreet support of the Jacobite cause made him a young man to watch. His very tactlessness may have persuaded them that he was not a serious cause of concern.

Savage continued to broadcast his views and Johnson sympathised with them. In Latin, he wrote a biting attack on Walpole. Savage made seditious talk exciting, for in the drab condition of his life Johnson was intoxicated by what Savage told him. What's more, in 1727 Savage had gained notoriety when, after a scuffle in a coffee house near Charing Cross, he had wounded a maid and killed a man. He had been charged with murder, put on trial – the case was so riveting that Pope came up from Twickenham to take notes – and found guilty.

A skilfully mounted campaign to release him made use of the services of the Earl of Tyrconnel, who was not on good terms with his aunt, Lady Macclesfield, and seems to have led the Countess of Hertford to appeal to the one intelligent and powerful member of the royal family, Queen Caroline. Savage was granted a royal pardon. He had been a lesser poet, a charlatan, and a fantasist. In an age that was fascinated by crime, by Newgate as a prison and Tyburn as the place of execution, it was only a few years since the

Caroline of Ansbach, King George II's intelligent consort

petty thief Jack Sheppard had become a popular hero for cheating the hangman so often by his skill as an escapologist. Now, Savage was notorious too.

With his sense of history, Johnson was impressed that Savage had been a friend of Sir Richard Steele and knew Pope. Savage also befriended the poet James Thomson, one of the Scotsmen who, after the 1707 Act of Union with England and Wales, came south to make a name and – with luck – a fortune.

Unlike Savage, Thomson gained lasting renown as author of 'The Seasons' which for a century taught readers how to appreciate landscape, until his vision was supplanted by William Wordsworth's. Today he is remembered as the man who wrote the words of a patriotic song to a tune by Arne in *Alfred the Great*, an entertainment staged in 1740 for the Prince and Princess of Wales at their country retreat, Cliveden in Buckinghamshire:"When Britain first, at Heaven's command,/ Arose from out the azure main, /This was the charter of her land,/ And guardian angels sung the strain:/ Rule, Britannia! Britannia rules the waves!/ Britons never shall be slaves."[24]

This was a declaration of Patriot sentiment, a repudiation of Danish invaders and, by implication, of invaders from Hanover.

Johnson met Thomson through Savage and their acquaintance lasted for about two years in the late 1730s. In the small hours they traipsed round smart streets in the West End, putting the

Georgian world to rights. 'Johnson has told me,' Sir John Hawkins recounted, 'that whole nights have been spent by him and Savage in conversations of this kind' not in a tavern, where they could have been warm and drunk some wine, but 'in a perambulation round the squares of Westminster, St James's in particular, when all the money they could both raise was less than sufficient to purchase for them the shelter and sordid comforts of a night shelter.' Hawkins went on to assert that these conversations 'gave rise to those principles of patriotism, that both, for some years after, avowed.'[25]

Johnson did not know that Savage had been a subject of government investigations, or how Savage had attacked in published writings the huge sums made by the East India Company trading in silks and spices at the natives' expense and by West India merchants trading in African slaves. Savage had poured scorn on imperial idealism, but nothing in Savage ever reached the grandeur of Pope in full flight. Savage's concerns are only of interest to the student of dissent in 18th century literature. Savage had a hopeless attachment to the Jacobite cause, but he appears sympathetic now for his distrust of British belligerance in foreign affairs and his loathing of slavery. Johnson knew his friend was just a minor poet and yet it seems that through Savage he became intent on retaining for the rest of his life Savage's hatred of the careless enjoyment of wealth without a thought for those through whose sufferings the wealth had been accumulated.

In 1744, Pope died and Swift, far away in Dublin, was already suffering from dementia. The man whose reputation they had worked to destroy, Sir Robert Walpole, had gone in 1742. The Patriot war against Spain had merged with a larger European war involving the Austrian succession and a colonial war against France that straddled Canada and India – and nothing was settled except that King George got his wish to be a British king to fight in battle. He was to be the last and he fought only once, but the fighting made sense of his favourite pastime: designing uniforms for his soldiers.

In July 1739, Savage had left for Wales, from where he moved to Bristol and by 1740 he was no longer a part of Johnson's life. Early in 1743, he was arrested for a debt of eight pounds and claimed that he had only threepence halfpenny, £7.19s.8 1/2d, short of what he needed. He was confined to Bristol Newgate. There, he abused the sickly Pope, who had treated him with constant kindness, and in August Savage died. Until his end, he railed against the world, disappointed that nobody cared for his play on a celebrated scandal at the court of James I, *The Murder of Sir Thomas Overbury*, furious that his aristocratic connections had not been adequately rewarded, but grateful that in his gaoler he had found a considerate friend. On his deathbed he wished to make some last confession, but before he made it he was dead.

Literary historians see the 1740s as a period of the flowering of a new art form: the novel. Twenty years earlier, Daniel Defoe had turned from reporting to writing a series of imaginary tales: among them *The Adventures of Robinson Crusoe*, *Moll Flanders* and *A Journal of the Plague Year*. He had no successors until Samuel Richardson revealed in *Pamela* how a good girl could reform a bad squire by resisting his advances until he offered marriage. It was a masterpiece of psychological observation, but the hypocrisy of it all, as he saw it, riled Henry Fielding. With his own training in farce, while training for the bar, he dashed off *Shamela*, the story of how by clever use of her 'vartue' a contriving minx traps a man of higher social status into an unsuitable match. Not content with sending up Richardson, Fielding then wrote a wonderful novel of his own, *Joseph Andrews*. Curiously, even though Johnson shared the same sort of education as Fielding – who had been educated at Eton – Johnson preferred the work of Richardson.

To the literature of the 1740s, Johnson's contribution was unique: *The Life of Mr Richard Savage*, which appeared within weeks of its subject's death, invented a new kind of biography that nobody but he, as yet, could develop: a life of a poet that dwelt on the poems as well as the life. The story he had to tell was sensational. It combined romance with the trappings of low life. He could point to aristocratic perfidy, see his hero dicing with death, rescued by royal sympathy, misled by vaulting ambition and finally enduring a pathetic end. Johnson used his forensic gifts to defend Savage's most indefensible actions, as in that coffee-house near Charing Cross, for he was in thrall to Savage's one supreme skill: his mastery of the art of self-dramatisation. Gone from his writing were the classical models, gone was any cautious research, for he had not bothered to check up on the facts that Savage had outlined. Johnson wrote out of love. How could anyone, after reading the story of Savage, presume to say, *Had I been in Savage's condition, I should have lived better or written better than Savage.*[26] It was a reflection that challenged his readers.

Johnson too wished to hold up a mirror to London life, to moralise on what he saw reflected in the glass, to make his readers wise, but instead he was charmed to forget his own plight by a wild dreamer in Grub Street. He came to his senses. He still had not provided adequately for Tetty. He no longer went on nightly prowls with Savage. He must find work that would pay.

The making of Dictionary Johnson • 1745–1755

By conviction a Tory and by sentiment a Jacobite, Johnson was stirred by the dramatic events of 1745. In that year, the eyes of the politicians were fixed north of the border on the last and greatest of the Jacobite rebellions. When the Stuart army came as far south as the city of Derby, George II was ready to flee to Hanover. In Scotland many years later, Johnson was delighted to talk with Jacobite sympathisers, but his sympathies had limits. He was a realist and though some have imagined that he either went north to fight for Bonnie Prince Charlie or went underground in London to spy on his behalf, he admitted to Boswell that *if holding up his right hand would have secured victory at Culloden to Prince Charles's army, he was not sure he would hold it up.*[27]

Power fell into the hands of the Pelham brothers: the prodigiously wealthy Duke of Newcastle and his colourless, shrewd younger brother, Henry. George II would have liked to have in government Carteret (later Earl Granville), as Carteret spoke German and appreciated the love that the King felt for Hanover – he was willing to campaign aggressively in Hanover's defence – but Pelham forced Carteret out and forced the King to back down by staging for the first time in English history a mass resignation of a ministry.

Pelham's administration was nicknamed the broad-bottomed government because it could include any kind of Whig but he did set limits: he stood for an easy-going way of life and nothing should get in its way. In 1748, he made peace at Aix-la-Chapelle–

to celebrate the event, Handel wrote his famous firework music – and the government made cuts in defence and taxation. After the collapse of the 1745 Jacobite rebellion and the pacification of Scotland, England enjoyed a period of dull stability. In other words, it was a good moment to embark on a grand project. Thus, Johnson drew up a plan for a dictionary of English.

The second half of 1745 and the beginning of 1746 was not a good time for him. At some stage in that period he tried to be admitted to practise law but was told that without a degree this was impossible. His hack journalism demonstrated his extraordinary versatility and yet, being ephemeral, was quickly forgotten.

Johnson was aware that he had done little to make Tetty proud of him. He could not offer her financial security or social status or companionship, indeed her small world of family and friends had been wrenched from her and nothing put in its place. Her sons still did not wish to see her and she lived many miles from her daughter, who loyally supported old Mrs Johnson in the bookshop. Tetty stayed in bed and went on drinking. The one consolation Sam could offer was a grand idea.

The idea had been suggested to him some years before by Robert Dodsley, an imaginative bookseller, but at that time he had abruptly rejected it. In 1746, Dodsley brought up the matter again, and this time Johnson went away to think about it. By April he had worked out a scheme, to be considered by whoever might be interested. Eventually seven booksellers – Dodsley, Andrew Millar, Charles Hitch, John Knapton, Paul Knapton, Thomas Longman and his nephew – signed a contract with him at breakfast in Holborn on 18 June. For £1,575, Johnson was to produce a dictionary in three years, on the assumption that he would do no other writing. The assumption must have seemed odd to anyone who knew Johnson, as he could not bear to be confined to one task. Moreover, neither he nor his backers understood how exacting was the labour he had set himself. He would take nine years and to hurry him up the booksellers advanced £100 more than they had originally proffered. When the job was done, they went carefully through the accounts, while they thanked Johnson with a dinner in his honour.

The signing of the contract enabled Johnson to find lodgings in which he could work. He needed a house for a team of amanuenses to work with him, and where he and Tetty could live.

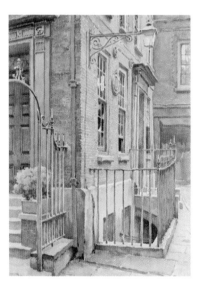

He found one at 17 Gough Square, a building that has become a Johnson museum equal in importance to his family home, the birthplace, in Lichfield. The house may seem large for a man who hitherto had been regarded as poor, but to accomplish what he had promised he needed ample working space. Above the floors where Johnson and Tetty lived there is a large garret, where Johnson's helpers worked at desks like those used in a counting house or, as we would say, at an accountant's. This room seems to have been littered with books,

Johnson's house on Gough Square remains unchanged today

papers and rickety furniture; it was Johnson's factory, where he and his team could fashion their masterwork without interference from guests or the women of the household.

A lot is known about Johnson's working methods. As always, he rose late to have breakfast before climbing up to the attic. He would start the process by reading through a volume by an author he admired, when he would mark a passage where he thought the author used a word or, sometimes several words, in an apt and accurate way. He would then underline the word or words in pencil, indicate where the passage he wished to quote began and ended, mark the appropriate letter in the margin and hand the book over to an assistant, who would transcribe what Johnson had selected. In the published *Dictionary*, there are mistakes in some of the quotations and this may have been the result of inattention on the part of one of his assistants or else Johnson's own fault – for example, sometimes he cites the wrong play by Shakespeare, the writer he quotes the most often – or deliberate design – sometimes he seems to have misquoted on purpose, a fact he admitted in his later *Preface*.

Like many editors and critics of the time, he did not doubt that texts could be improved. He had a genius for compression that he did not hesitate to use, for he aimed always to be readable. He had a theory of English usage that already by the mid-18th century was going to cause trouble. In his *Preface*, he laid down the principle that had dictated his choice of quotations: *I have fixed Sidney's work for the boundary, beyond which I make few excursions. From the authors who arose in the time of Elizabeth, a speech might be formed adequate to all the purposes of use and elegance. If the language of theology were extracted from Hooker and the translation of the Bible; the terms of natural knowledge from Bacon; the phrases of policy, war and navigation from Raleigh ; the dialect of poetry and fiction from Sidney and Spenser; and the diction of common life from Shakespeare, few ideas would be lost to mankind, for want of English words, in which they might be expressed.*[28]

For Johnson, the late Elizabethan age was, therefore, a golden age in the use of the language, yet he knew that since then the language had changed. He made it a rule to use modern spelling even when it was misleading, as when he allowed *gibberish* instead of *gebrish*, which means *the jargon of Geber*.[29] He wanted to fix pronunciation on rational grounds but had to admit that *generous* had only two syllables and that *great* sometimes rhymes with *state*, as it does today, and sometimes with *seat*, as it does no longer. In 'Epistle to Arbuthnot', Pope's satirical portrait of Addison-as-

Atticus, he rhymed 'obliged' with 'besieged' and in the Romance part of the language, as in Chaucer's day, the words derived from French usually still betrayed their French origin in their sound as well as in their look. A word that was Teutonic, however, had often retained a Teutonic spelling, but was pronounced in a way that no longer made clear its etymology, so that in *name* the final *e* had become mute, like the guttural sound *gh* and Johnson had to admit that this, the oldest English section of the language caused him problems. He was forced to compare many such words with modern Dutch or German words, as linguistic *sisters*.[30] Of course, Johnson was dead before the 19th century linguists uncovered the common roots of Indo-European tongues; he knew nothing of Grimm's law that could explain connections between an ancient Greek and a modern English form, and he lived in a time when 'Gothic' or 'Gothick' was a term of aesthetic abuse or an aesthetic fad, not the obsolete tongue into which Bishop Ulfilas had translated the Bible for barbarian tribes.

Johnson was aware that the English were late in having a dictionary. In Italy, the Academia della Crusca, dating back to 1585, had tried to regulate the Italian tongue as other academies had laid down rules for music or literature or science. And, when Cardinal Richelieu founded the Académie française in 1635, he intended that its illustrious members should limit anarchy in French speech and writing as he had forced nobles to acknowledge the authority of the French king.

Notoriously, compilers of the French dictionary had taken a long time to reach the end of the letter 'A' and its 40 members had taken 40 years to complete their Dictionary. Meanwhile, Johnson proposed to finish his work in just three years. When challenged on the topic, he remarked: *Let me see; forty times forty is sixteen hundred. As three to sixteen hundred, so is the proportion of a Frenchman to an Englishman.*[31]

It would be misleading, however, to think that he did not

begin until 1746. Subconsciously, Johnson had been studying the meaning of words from childhood. At home he had been surrounded by books. His mastery of Latin at an early age had given him an acute sense of the underrated art of translation. He had had his nose – his poor eyesight meant he had to put books close to his face – in dictionaries like the Arab-Latin dictionary of the Dutch scholar Joseph Scaliger, especially when in the 1740s he worked in the Harleian library.

For Johnson the experience of browsing in a first-class library proved to be a superb preparation for a lexicographer. While perusing rare books, he gained information on etymologies, thought about definitions and came across models for his future venture. Latin-Latin dictionaries, like that of the Frenchman Robert Estienne (at that time anglicised as 'Stephens' but nowadays English scholars use his French name) taught him to value the judicious use of illustrative quotation. But for all his debt to Latin and his awareness that since the 16th-century English had incorporated more Latin words, he was certain that English was at root a Germanic tongue. Lord Chesterfield, nominal patron of his *Dictionary*, hoped English would be more Latinate, but this project was bound to be hopeless. English grammar has no Latin or Romance habits: its nouns have no gender and no cases, its verbs scarcely conjugate and, when they are used in a verbal function, its prepositions stand

Robert Harley led Queen Anne's Tory government from 1710 to 1714. Harley was a bibliophile and had assembled a collection of books and pamphlets on English history in addition to many manuscripts.

In 1753, Harley's granddaughter sold the manuscripts to Parliament and they were transferred to the British Museum in 1757. Meanwhile, the books and pamphlets were purchased by the publisher Thomas Osborne, who had intended to sell them on. He thought he would make more money if he could produce a catalogue of the collection and co-opted Johnson, who had a reputation as a fast worker, to produce it.

apart from the verb whose sense they modify (as in 'wash up' or 'wash down').

As Thomas Osborne was to learn, Johnson was no push-over. It occurred while Johnson was working on the *Harleian Miscellany*, a name given to the set of pamphlets he was editing. Sometimes out of curiosity he would read more than his job required, and Osborne, furious at Johnson's waywardness, shouted at him abusively. When Johnson, who was reading quickly, said his delay was necessary, Osborne accused him of lying. At this, Johnson grabbed an enormous 16th-century Greek Bible, swung it at Osborne, knocked him over, put his foot on Osborne's neck and told him to get up slowly in case he would be kicked downstairs. After that, Osborne remonstrated with him no longer and between 1744 and 1746, the *Miscellany* was published in instalments.

In occasional moments until spring 1745, Johnson continued helping Cave to edit *The Gentlemen's Magazine*, and he published a brief essay on *Macbeth*. When, therefore, he promised to work on the *Dictionary*, Johnson was both well-prepared to fulfil the commission and had no reason to suspect he would not have enough time to concentrate on what he had promised to do.

Discussion about defining and refining the language had been a favourite topic in the circle of Pope and Swift. Pope had made a list of authors to be consulted and Swift had drafted a *Proposal for Correcting, Improving and Ascertaining the English Language*. Johnson did not follow the advice of Swift, whom he heartily disliked, on correcting and improving, but he found Pope's suggestions invaluable – except when they clashed with his principles.

Like many of his predecessors – including Joseph Scaliger, the Dutch scholar – he thought that the study of words must have an educational aim: the moral and religious betterment of the reader. This seems to be why he omitted from his approved authors Pope's friend Viscount Bolingbroke (1678–1751), as he was not a believing Christian. Johnson may have had some respect for such a man – after all, it was thanks to Bolingbroke that Pope had imitated Horace to attack Walpole, a device Johnson had copied with his use of Juvenal in 'London' – but he drew the line when he thought the Christian religion was at stake. Bolingbroke was openly a Deist, one who believed in a god known by reason alone, like a celestial watchmaker, not in the God who is revealed to faith and, therefore, he would not treat the works of Bolingbroke as canonical. He also allowed himself a crack at Bolingbroke when he defined irony as *A mode of speech in which the meaning is contrary to the words: as, 'Bolingbroke was a* pious *man.'*[33]

Another famous prose writer on Pope's list and not on Johnson's was Thomas Hobbes, a greater philosopher than Bolingbroke but one whom Johnson believed taught immorality. He viewed Hobbes as a determinist whose views undermined the belief in freedom of choice and action, and on the subject of freedom he drew examples from Milton, a poet

While Johnson always revered Dryden and Pope, his reaction to Pope's friend Jonathan Swift (1667–1745) was problematic. In his early career, he had used Swift's device of comparing contemporary politicians to the little people of Lilliput, but when he later wrote about *Gulliver's Travels* oddly he criticised the book for its incredible stories.[32] Swift's genius was too quirky for Johnson, and he was probably shocked by Swift's fondness for scatological humour and the way he treated women.

whose republican politics Johnson hated. Yet he does not quote, as a modern reader might expect, from Milton's plea for freedom of speech in *Areopagitica*. Instead, he cites only Milton's essay 'Of Education'. He took a special interest in similar books, whether by John Locke, Isaac Watts or, tellingly, by Elizabeth I's tutor, Roger Ascham, whose 1570 *Schoolmaster* fits just inside the chronological frame of reference he had set. A failed schoolmaster himself, in writing his *Dictionary* he was proving for all time what a great educator he could be.

Though Johnson wished to ennoble language, he was conscious that words may be used carelessly and that, therefore, he must respect popular usage. He anchored the word *ruin* in its Latin source, the verb *ruo* (I fall), but he drifted with the tide when he defined *mild* by its synonyms and antonyms as *kind, tender, good, indulgent, merciful, compassionate, clement, soft, not severe, not cruel.*[34]

In this spirit, Johnson balanced his own orotund Latinity against the pithy linguistic tradition handed down from the Anglo-Saxons. This gave him another reason to dislike Bolingbroke, whose long exile in France had made him use his native tongue in a Frenchified way. While discussing Bolingbroke's fifth use of *to owe*, Johnson commented: *A practice has long prevailed among writers, to use* owing, *the active participle of* owe *in a passive sense....Bolingbroke....having no quick sense of the force of English words, has used* due *in the sense of consequence or imputation...We say, the money is* due *to me; Bolingbroke says, the effect is* due *to the cause.*[35]

Johnson sought English pure and undefiled; he found a language with its own distinct rules, the chief one of which is that it was a language full of exceptions. Only a true-born Englishman knew them. He was proud to state in his *Preface*: *it may gratify curiosity to inform it, that the* English Dictionary *was written with little assistance of the learned, and without any patronage of the great; not in the soft obscurities of retirement, or under the shelter of academic bowers, but amidst inconvenience and distraction, in sickness and sorrow; and it may repress the triumph of malignant criticism to observe that, if our language is not here fully displayed, I have only failed in an attempt which no human powers have hitherto completed.*[36]

Today, much of the *Dictionary* serves largely as an introduction to late-18th century usage, so a novel (in Italian a *novella*) is *A small tale, generally of love.*[37] Right from the start, however, what drew attention were his idiosyncratic definitions. A *lexicographer* is *A writer of dictionaries; a harmless drudge.*[38] *Oats* is *A grain, which in England is generally given to horses, but in Scotland supports the people.*[39] He was almost prosecuted for libel because he maintained that *excise*, a recent and unpopular tax that had almost brought down Walpole in 1733, was *A hateful tax levied upon commodities, and adjudged not by the common judges of property, but wretches hired by those to whom excise is paid.*[40] Two such definitions had a personal resonance. A *pension* – the definition would haunt him – *is generally understood to mean pay given to a state hireling for treason to his country.*[41]

At the time, he was more concerned with the qualities of a *patron*, deemed *a wretch who supports with insolence, and is paid with flattery,*[42] for whatever he said he was thinking of Lord Chesterfield. It had been Dodsley's idea to ask Chesterfield to support the grand enterprise and Chesterfield had given Johnson £10 and then done nothing more to help him. He had forgotten about the matter and was perhaps pleasantly surprised to find the *Dictionary* was dedicated to him. Touchy as ever, Johnson had made efforts to keep the noble lord informed of his progress, but the noble lord had other suitors, other concerns. So, while the great work was in its final stages with the printers, Johnson decided to strike back. He drafted a letter to Chesterfield who, glad to show that he bore no grudge for appearing to be ungracious, left the letter out, so that visitors waiting to see him could read it. In this way, the letter became celebrated. It deserves to be

Dr Samuel Johnson kept waiting in the ante-room of his patron lord
Chesterfield, a detail from the painting by E M Ward

so, for it has a marvellous rhythm. *Seven years, My lord have passed
since I waited in your outward rooms or was repulsed from your door,
during which time I have been pushing through my work, through
difficulties of which it is useless to complain, and have brought it
to the verge of publication, without one act of assistance, one word of
encouragement, or one smile of favour. Such treatment I did not expect, for
I never had a patron before.*[43]

The letter was written on 7 February 1755, and *A Dictionary
of the English Language* published on 15 April. While Johnson may
not have had any help from Lord Chesterfield, he had been sustained by his ability to cope with a host of distractions – some of
them of his own making – one of them tragic.

The year 1749 had been wonderful, for reasons that had nothing
to do with his lexicographical labours. Thanks to Garrick,
Johnson had at last the satisfaction of seeing *Irene*, the tragedy on

which he had set such store, acted at Garrick's theatre, Drury Lane. Garrick took the trouble to provide the play with a fine cast, magnificent costumes and an exotic scenery befitting its eastern setting. He faced down hisses and catcalls and, although he made a mistake in trying to present the strangulation of the heroine on stage, he made the first night enough of a success to carry on for nine nights, so that Johnson could enjoy the three author's benefit nights. He earned £195 and, by selling the text to Dodsley for a further £100, pocketed more in days than before in a year. He was a nuisance at rehearsals, he found the actresses ill-educated and sexually tempting and he never wrote another drama. Only a week or so earlier, for 15 guineas he had sold to Dodsley the copyright of the first poem to which he had fixed his name: 'The Vanity of Human Wishes', loosely based on Juvenal's tenth satire.

Neoclassical critics considered satire a hybrid art, a halfway house between comedy and tragedy. In Johnson's case, the natural tendency of his imagination was towards tragedy. Juvenal combined rage, fun and derision in a way that only one of his English followers has managed to mimic closely – and that poet was Dryden, who had translated him. Johnson's imitation was like a noble variation on Juvenal's racy themes. Johnson was discreet when his model was scatological and, though English is more concrete than Latin, he breathed a rarefied air of abstraction, until the reader scrutinises his lines. From the opening paragraph, he balanced generalised ideas against particular images:

Then say how hope and fear, desire and hate,
O'er spread with snares the clouded maze of fate,
Where wavering man, betrayed by venturous pride,
To tread the dreary paths without a guide;
As treacherous phantoms in the mist delude,
Shuns fancied ills, or chases airy good.[44]

He had a talent for concision of which Juvenal, the author of lively jingles such as *'mens sana in corpore sano'*[45] (a healthy mind in a healthy body) and neat phrases like '*panem et circenses*'[46] (bread and circuses), would have approved. But with Johnson there was an added note of moral earnestness derived from his own bitter experience. Whereas Juvenal jeered at life's losers, including himself, Johnson was stirred by life's unfairness. He was good at fitting modern equivalents to ancient examples, so that Sejanus, the favourite brought down by his master Tiberius, was easily transmuted into Wolsey, the favourite brought down by his master Henry VIII. But if Juvenal was interested only in the rapidity and surprise element in his fall, Johnson pitied the man whose *last sighs reproach the faith of Kings*.[47] His Hannibal was also apt. Charles XII of Sweden, who had won one daring campaign after another, ventured far into Russia, had his army annihilated on the snowy fields of Pultava and with his reputation for invincibility shot to pieces, was reduced to becoming a mere excuse for sententious reflection:

> *He left the name, at which the world grew pale*
> *To point a moral, or adorn a tale.*[48]

Both are equally harsh on those who yearn for a long life, Juvenal is funnier on the varied sexual fates of the good looking, but Johnson rises more easily to grandeur. At the start he had undertaken a universal theme, with the injunction to *Survey mankind, from China to Peru*[49] and at the end he recommended a universal solution to mankind's ills: *Pour forth thy fervours for a healthful mind,/ Obedient passions and a will resigned..../ With these celestial wisdom calms the mind,/ And makes the happiness she does not find.*[50]

Even Johnson needed to relax and in 1750 he thought up an idea for a money-spinner: he would produce two essays a week. From that March of that year until March 1752, he published *The Rambler*, almost without aid. He was conscious that he was joining a great European tradition. In the 16th century, the Dutch scholar Erasmus wished to illustrate the meaning of famous Latin tags so he devised a system of discussing them briefly in his clear, elegant style. These became known wherever and by whomever he was read – and he was read all over Europe by priests, professors, schoolmasters, pupils and men of letters.

In France, the nobleman Michel de Montaigne wished to give Erasmus's public invention a private meaning. He asked himself, '*Que sçais-je*' or 'What do I know?' His answer was: only himself, but himself illuminated by the learning of the past. His attempts, called *essais*, were translated into English and an Englishman, Francis Bacon, developed the concept in a more impersonal style. Bacon's *Essays* examined general ideas, such as truth, or general topics, such as gardens – the reader never discovers much about Bacon's intimate life – and these were read throughout the 17th century, not least because he was seen as a prophet of the new science.

In the early 18th century, the form was revived by the Whig journalists Addison and Steele but in their case they were writing for a new audience of ladies and gentlemen. That did not mean they did not discuss serious matters – Addison was the first critic to analyse at length the poetry of Milton – but they

Johnson admired Addison as a writer but had little sympathy with his Whig politics. Nothing indicates this so clearly as the contrasting ways in which he defined the differences between the words 'Whig and Tory'. Whig was *(1) Whey (2) The name of a faction. One of our unhappy terms of division*. By contrast, a Tory was *One who adheres to the ancient constitution of the state and the apostolic hierarchy of the Church of England, as opposed to Whig.*

hit on a more popular note when they invented the character of Sir Roger de Coverley, a Tory squire. The name came from the country dance, which lasted into the 20th century, but Addison's easy manner converted what was meant to be a satirical portrait of the typical supporter of the other side into a loveable eccentric, who would stand up in church on Sundays to see which parishioners were present. Yet readers simpered when Sir Roger died.

Johnson wished to combine various features of the traditional essay: mottos, the digressive tone, the occasional earnestness, the gentle touch. He had Latin phrases for the mottos in his head and he loved arguing a case. Gravity was natural to him but he could be humorous, too. He meant his five essays on Milton to compete with Addison. His concern with the new romantic fiction – he was a friend of Richardson, author of *Pamela* and *Clarissa* – showed him as up-to-date and he put in a word for biography, of which he would be a master. He could identify an important issue and for *Rambler* 60, he drafted an impassioned attack on capital punishment – the 18th-century penal code was harsh – and in *Rambler* 148 he denounced paternal cruelty. He also showed some sympathy with the lot of women and invented a series of imaginary ladies, some of dubious quality, to grumble about their lives. 'Misella', a prostitute, was granted *Rambler* 170 and 171, 'Zosima' revealed the social indignities suffered by a gentlewoman forced to be a servant and 'Myrtilla' spoke of her horror at learning about domestic tyranny.

The *Rambler* essays did not earn Johnson as much money as he had hoped, but in an age when copyright law was still unsatisfactory, they made a lot of provincial newspaper editors happy as pirated editions soon appeared in Bath, Bristol, Leeds, Newcastle, Nottingham and Salisbury. Collections of the essays kept them before the gaze of the reading public for 50 or 60 years, until Johnson's popularity began to wane.

Johnson stopped writing his essays abruptly. The solicitude he had taken over the concerns of his imaginary women correspondents was harder to display in the case of Tetty. When not busy with the *Rambler* on Monday and Friday evenings, or erratically on the *Dictionary*, or every Tuesday evening with friends of the Ivy Lane Club, he made little time for his wife. Much of the day she was bedridden, often drugged or drunk, and when he saw her, she was full of complaints. A romantic attachment had lost its attractions.

The last *Rambler,* in which he discussed poverty, sickness and death, came out on 14 March. In the night of the 17th/18th, Tetty died. She was buried in Bromley, Kent, in a woollen shroud, as the law prescribed, after Johnson had removed her ring. For reasons that only he knows, he did not attend her funeral, he did not bring himself to visit her grave for a year and he did not put up a tombstone for her for 32 years.

Frank Barber

The Dictionary contained a long entry on opium, her drug. With the death of Tetty, Johnson's circumstances changed. New people joined the house in Gough Square: Miss Williams, who was almost blind; and Francis or 'Frank' Barber, a black boy who had been a slave. In written prayers, Johnson begged God for forgiveness: he would be kind. Soon to be famous, now a widower, he was free to become a man about town.

The discontents of Rasselas • 1755–1760

The death of Henry Pelham in 1754 led to a period of political instability. For nearly a decade he had run the government with his elder bother, the Duke of Newcastle, arranging the votes. But now the Duke was in a quandary. He alone had the cash to buy enough votes in the House of Commons whenever the government needed them, but he lacked the decisiveness to run a government.

However, there was one politician with the opposite problem. William Pitt (1708–78) was sure that he alone knew how to run a government but he had neither the money nor the patience to win and keep supporters. During peacetime, such a state of affairs would not have worried many in the sleepy world of 18th-century politics. But in India there had been a state of continuous warfare between the East India Company and the French Compagnie des Indes, and in America a war had just broken out between the English and French colonists. On the continent, three powerful ladies, Elizabeth, Tsarina of Russia, Maria Theresa, Queen-Empress of Hungary and Austria, and Madame de Pompadour, the official mistress of Louis XV of France, found that they shared a common aim: to destroy Frederick, King of Prussia. Commercial interests in the City stood to become enormously wealthy if the East India Company could outsmart its French rival, and while for most politicians the English priority was the defeat of the French in North America, especially after a humiliating defeat in 1755.

Yet even the most narrowly patriotic of Englishmen could see it did not pay England, let alone Hanover, were Prussia to be overwhelmed so that France and Austria (ruler of Belgium) would hold the shores across the Channel. Thus, Pitt and Newcastle had to combine their talents to provide the country with a ministry capable of fighting a complex war. The old King, George II, had long hated Pitt for his past attacks on the Hanoverian connection, but he

Samuel Johnson drawing from a portrait by Reynolds

came to realise that he needed Pitt just as much as Pitt needed him. In the end, after months and months of frustration, the King got a ministry that could win campaigns abroad and votes at home, one of the most successful governments in English history. He ended his reign on a note of triumph.

Johnson did not feel like fighting his own battles. The writing of the *Dictionary* had made him internationally famous, but it had not given him a steady income. Mentally exhausted, he found it hard to come up with another scheme that would bring him money. Twice in the five years between 1755 and 1760 he was imprisoned for debt. Both times, he was confident that his friends would obtain his release and he turned out to be right. On the first occasion he contacted the novelist Samuel Richardson who immediately provided more than the money he had to produce. On the second occasion he appealed to the publisher Jacob Tonson whom he had interested in a plan to edit an edition of Shakespeare's plays. Once again, he was saved but he had been humiliated without having found a lasting remedy to prevent the same situation from recurring.

Socially, he was isolated and instinctively he began to look for new acquaintances. There was no Tetty at home, he had to plan to leave Gough Square, which was in a squalid state, and he was short of companionship as the Ivy Lane Club dissolved. Hawkins, who is the main source of information about it, married well and preferred to stay at home. Others were dead or dying or no longer appeared at the King's Head Tavern.

There was a further cause of distress. One of his young friends, the poet Christopher 'Kit' Smart (1722–71), broke down in 1756 and began a rapid descent into madness, suffering from religious mania. It was of him that Johnson declared: *He insisted on people praying with him; and I'd as lief* (willingly) *pray with Kit Smart as any one else. Another charge was, that he did not love clean linen; and I have no passion for it.*[51]

According to Boswell, these remarks were made to Charles Burney, a fine organist later celebrated as the ablest musicologist in England and father of the novelist Fanny, who was much taken with *The Rambler* essays and still more by *The Dictionary*. He wrote to Johnson from Norfolk to ask how he could acquire a copy of the *Dictionary* for himself. He was one of the first of a group of able men that in the middle and late 1750s came to cluster round Johnson like satellites round a planet. Another was Thomas Warton, Fellow of Trinity College Oxford, who had sent Johnson a copy of his book on Spenser's *Faerie Queene*. A third, Thomas Percy, later a bishop, researched even more avidly than Warton the byways of medieval literature and rediscovered ballads before the Romantics.

Johnson also got on well with much younger men, two of whom would remain dear to him for the rest of his life. The first, Bennet Langton (1737–1801), had contacted him while still a schoolboy. Langton was a formidable Greek scholar even in his adolescence and, though he was dismayed by Johnson's appearance until he heard the great man speak, Johnson was immediately taken by the obvious intelligence of the gentleman before him.

The other young friend was more surprising. At Oxford, Langton was attracted to Topham Beauclerck, (1739–80) a handsome rake with an amusing, malicious tongue and an endless fund of charm. Johnson was favourably impressed. While there was only one very famous member of the Langton family, the archbishop who was largely responsible for drafting the Magna Carta, Beauclerck was an aristocrat, a great-grandson of Charles II and his most appealing mistress, Nell Gwynne.

Despite his love life, Charles II was Johnson's favourite Stuart, *the last English monarch who was a man of parts.*[52] Johnson could not endorse Beauclerck's behaviour but he came to love him. *Thy body is all vice,* he once told him*, and thy mind is all virtue.*[53] Shortly after Langton introduced Johnson to Beauclerck, the two sat up until three o'clock in the morning drinking in a London tavern. On a whim they called on Johnson and woke him up. He prepared to defend himself with a poker, until he saw who his callers were and decided to join them. *I'll have a frisk with you,*[54] he said, so he dressed and walked round town with them, stopping off to help the fruit and vegetable stallholders in Covent Garden, then to drink punch in a tavern and so to have themselves rowed downstream to the fish market at Billingsgate, where Langton left to keep a breakfast appointment with some young ladies. Beauclerck and Johnson carried on with the 'frolic' all day long. When Garrick heard of it, he told Johnson he would be in the gossip columns. Meanwhile, Johnson commented that Garrick would love to have done the same but did not dare do so because of his wife.

None of these friends mattered quite so much to him as a man of whose chosen profession Johnson had little comprehension. Joshua Reynolds (1723–92) came from a long line of clerics and

A portrait of Topham Beauclerck, one of Johnson's boon companions

academics, fellows of colleges at Oxford, Cambridge and Eton. In this family he was unique, for he chose to paint. He apprenticed in London with a passable painter named Thomas Hudson and there his social ease made him an agreeable member of a group of artists and writers who met at Slaughter's Coffee House in St Martin's Lane, near to the St Martin's Lane Academy, an institution revived by William Hogarth to promote native, English as opposed to foreign, French art. Occasionally, Henry Fielding and David Garrick would drop in to entertain the painters.

Reynolds lodged nearby in St Martin's Lane, until the death of his father obliged him to go home. A lucky occurrence prevented him from being a purely provincial, even a purely English artist. Through the Edgcumbes, a local noble family, he was introduced to a naval officer, Augustus Keppel, who was passing through Devonport on his way to taking up a commission in the Mediterranean. Keppel and Reynolds got on, so Keppel asked him to accompany him. The aesthetic reward for Keppel was that early in the 1750s, Reynolds had painted a portrait of his friend striding along the shore. What the connoisseur would have noticed is that he depicted Keppel in the pose of a famous statue from the papal collection, the *Apollo Belvedere*. In 1750, Reynolds had gone ashore to begin a grand tour of the sites of Italy, starting with Rome. Unlike Hogarth, his predecessor, or Gainsborough, his future rival, Reynolds became learned in the grand art of ancient and modern Rome. So, his visual education was equivalent to Johnson's literary education. And he had an advantage: he had read Pliny on art in Latin.

While his painting of Keppel made Reynolds famous in the art world, in the literary world he achieved celebrity through his first meeting with Johnson, probably in 1756. Reynolds had read Johnson, but Johnson probably knew little about Reynolds until they met in the home of two Misses Cotterells, an admiral's maiden daughters. When they began to lament the death of a friend 'to whom,' according to Boswell, 'they had great obligations',[55] Reynolds commented that they had at least 'the comfort of being relieved from a burthen of gratitude'.[56] The ladies were shocked, but Johnson was pleased. Here was a man after his heart, who

said what was true, like the moralist François VI, Duc de la Rochefoucauld (1613–80), even if the truth hurt. The two men supped together, talked and talked, and talked themselves into being each other's closest friend. Reynolds was the master of ceremonies among Johnson's friends; Johnson acted as Reynolds's conscience.

Shortly after the meeting, Reynolds painted a portrait of Johnson, that he eventually gave to Boswell. Boswell's gift to

Johnson from an engraving by Heath

Reynolds was incomparable: he dedicated his *Life of Johnson* to the painter.

Johnson's friends amused and cheered him up, even saved him from prison, but they could not give him a job. Thus, Johnson had to return to occasional journalism. Several publishers asked him to run and supervise a new literary journal to be called *The Literary Magazine, or Universal Review*. The first number appeared in May 1756, by which time the Seven Years' War was under way. Almost at once, Johnson found himself at variance with the owners for, if he had not liked the French and Indian War, he disliked equally its European concomitant because he knew that in British eyes France was the worldwide enemy.

In British imperial history, the years 1755 and 1756 were full of disasters. In July 1755, General Braddock on his way to attack Fort Duquesne on the Ohio River was ambushed by a Franco-Indian force and killed. (Of his principal officers, the only important one to survive was a certain Virginian gentleman called George Washington.) In 1756, Siruj-ud-Daulah, Nawab of Bengal, sensing that the East India Company was preparing to attack the fort of their French rivals in Chandernagor, made a sudden attack on Fort William in Calcutta, took it and, legend says, his men then herded the surviving British soldiers into the so-called black hole of Calcutta. Closer to home was the incident when a well-advertised venture by the fleet of Toulon led to the capture of Minorca and the withdrawal of the British squadron under Admiral Byng.

Although later in life Johnson enjoyed a brief correspondence with Warren Hastings, the celebrated governor of Bengal, he was not much concerned with the exploits of Robert Clive in India, nor did he envy the enormous fortunes gained by 'nabobs' (as the East India Company men were called) – he preferred to earn less in England while enjoying a more pleasant style of life.

But the lands of America and Europe were abiding interests. In 1756, he wrote three essays on international relations: *An Introduction to the Political State of Great-Britain*; *Observations on the Present State of Affairs*; and *Observations on His Britannic Majesty's Treaties with Her Imperial Majesty of All the Russia's and the Landgrave of Hesse-Cassel.* He had no time for patriotic claptrap: in a discussion dated 1775, he told Boswell that *patriotism is the last refuge of a scoundrel.*[57]

Johnson's great enemy always was humbug, but in war time his natural tendency to be outspoken became embarrassing. He was shunted off to safer ground. For *The Literary Magazine* he reviewed books on a range of topics that even for him was amazing: theology, philosophy, geography, politics, history, warfare.

In his first, controversial political essay, he exposed the deep-seated reasons for the failures of a British colonial administration that led ultimately to Braddock's disastrous defeat. *A French governor is seldom chosen for any other reason than his qualifications for his trust. . . Their great security is the friendship of the natives, and to this they have an indubitable right; because it is the consequence of their virtue.* By contrast, *our planters are always quarreling with their governor, whom they consider are less to be trusted than the French; and our traders hourly alienate the Indians by their tricks and oppressions, and we continue to show every day by new proofs, that no people can be great who have ceased to be virtuous.*[58]

In the second essay, he was more even-handed, arguing the cases for and against the use of Russian and Hessian mercenaries before concluding that he would prefer an English militia to defend England.

In the third essay, the even-handedness led to a scathing onslaught on colonialism. *The American dispute between the French and us is therefore only a quarrel between two robbers for the spoils of a passenger.*[59]

Such sentiments might have been useful to those who wished to denigrate the unpopular administration of Newcastle, but when Pitt became War Minister and virtual Foreign Minister in 1757, the tone Johnson adopted seemed unacceptable. In 1758, his *Observations* showed how unenthusiastic he was about the war. On August 19: *Our troops have at last taken a French town; Cherbourg is in the possession of the English.*[60] On August 26: *Louisbourg is now taken, and our streets echo with triumph, and blaze with illumination, as if our King was once more proclaimed at Paris . . . Louisbourg is not useful to us in the same way in which its loss is detrimental to our enemies.*[61] On September 30: *we had no need, and made no use of the resolution shewn by the French in the attack on Minorca.*[62]

The grudging admissions of British successes revealed in these remarks did not endear Johnson to the proprietors of the magazine. Thus, they confined Johnson to the review pages. In any case, his judgements on global strategy proved to be premature.

The capture of Cherbourg was a prelude to the rout of the French navy off Quiberon Bay, that of Louisbourg prepared the way for the taking of Quebec, even the use of mercenary troops was vindicated by the victory of Minden. The year 1759 was Pitt's year of victories.

Johnson's chief concerns were still humanitarian causes. He agitated in favour of Admiral Byng, who was court-martialled and shot for abandoning Minorca. In 1760, he wrote a pamphlet in which he supported those who proposed generous treatment of French prisoners of war. *It is far from certain that a single Englishman will suffer by the charity to the French.*[63]

The Literary Magazine and occasional pamphlets did not make a career. He still had to eat. When he advertised his intention to edit Shakespeare, he had been blocked by the poetaster Hanmer and, to its shame, by the Clarendon Press.

In 1756, he promised that he would produce his version of the *Complete Works* within a year. He did work on the project during the late 1750s, but nothing was ready for the printers until 1765. Once again, he had been over-optimistic. His powers of concentration were remarkable but a rate of a week and a half for each play was beyond even his abilities to maintain. He had the self-knowledge to realise that he was at his best when he worked fast, but the sort of task suitable to a style of rapid composition was either an occasional essay or a theme about which he had thought long and hard.

Johnson's consistent attacks on British warfare and his evident dislike of all colonial adventures may seem odd to those who associate Toryism with the Empire and the armed forces. In fact, that Tory tradition was created by Benjamin Disraeli in the latter part of the 19th century. In the 18th century, the Tories tended to hate all wars except defensive ones and wars waged largely by the navy.

From 15 April 1758 to 5 April 1760, Johnson produced a

weekly piece entitled 'The Idler' for another magazine called *The Universal Chronicle*, specifically invented for the purpose of giving Johnson a platform. There were stock market reports and news summaries after his essay. It was the essay, however, that made the paper, and soon pirated versions of 'The Idler' were available in the provinces.

Johnson was no longer willing to cope with the strain of producing twice weekly articles, as in the days of *The Rambler*, and, although he wished to boost sales, he had no intention of bearing the burden of achieving commercial success alone. Once or twice he was able to turn to one of his new friends, to Thomas Warton, Bennet Langton or Joshua Reynolds, if he wanted someone else to take his place. What was immediately apparent was that he was aiming for a new lightness of touch in his style: the sentences had become shorter, there was no longer a classical quotation at the head of every essay, the choice of words was less Latinate and the mood often whimsical.

The gravity of manner typical of *The Rambler* crept back into several later essays, and on moral issues he was, as always, categorical. In the 11th essay, he tartly pointed out that *slavery is now no where more patiently endured, than in countries once inhabited by the zealots of liberty*.[64] And on the question of imprisonment for debt, on which he had very personal reasons for strong feelings, he maintained: *it is vain to continue an institution, which experience shows to be ineffectuall*.[65]

Johnson also smiled. Tom Tempest is *a steady friend to the house of Stuart . . . He believes that king William burned Whitehall* (Palace). His political counterpart, Jack Sneaker, supported the Hanoverian cause just as vehemently, so had known *those who saw the bed into which the Pretender was conveyed in a warming-pan*. He too was hourly disturbed by the dread of Popery, and everywhere he saw some French plot at work. He believed that *king William never lost a battle*.[66] Johnson and his readers knew that the opposite was the case, for in continental wars William III never won one.

The finest of these portraits came in his satire of professional critics. Johnson's viewpoint was established in his first sentence: *criticism is a study by which men grow important and formidable at very small expense.* 'Dick Minim', a weak scholar trained as a brewer but left well-off by the death of an uncle, disliked work so much that he frequents the theatre. He *did not trust so much to natural sagacity, as wholly to neglect the study of books.* He learnt by heart a few banal sayings: *the chief business of art is to copy nature*; *a perfect writer is not to be expected*; *the great art is the art of blotting.*[67] Minim gave passable marks to Shakespeare and Jonson, did not recommend Spenser's stanza or the rhyming couplets in Dryden's tragedies, censured Congreve for making all his characters witty, and degraded Pope from a poet to a versifier. As nobody contradicted him, he became certain he is right, he acquires a special seat in a coffee house, his coterie in the pit. He devises a plan to have an Academy of Criticism, where he will hold the Chair. The only author he can read with pleasure is Milton – and soon he is so admired that young men come to him for advice.

In 1688, James II's queen, Mary of Modena, gave birth to her only child, James Edward. The legend of the warming pan – that the baby boy had been swapped with the royal child by being brought in the warming pan into the royal bedchamber – was one way of proving that the son had no claim to the throne. In fact, the prince had not been smuggled into his mother's bed: as was normal, the birth there had been witnessed by the chief officers of state.

'Dick Minim' was a telling character because he was a parody of everything for which Johnson stood. Essentially, he was shallow and nothing made his inventor more furious than pretentious nonsense.

Two years earlier, Johnson had come across opinions he thought much more offensive than anything held by Dick Minim. In

1757, he was invited to review Soame Jenyns's *A Free Inquiry into the Nature and origins of Evil*. Jenyns's treatise was set out in six letters.

Johnson set out to refute them in three successive issues of *The Literary Magazine*. Johnson revered Pope as a poet, but he hated the thoughts Pope had expressed in his *Essay on Man*. Only too conscious himself of how hard life could be, he had no time for what a modern literary historian of ideas, Basil Willey, calls the 'cosmic Toryism'[68] implied in the famous aphorism: Whatever is, is Right.[69]

Jenyns's second letter *on the evils of imperfection*, Johnson wrote, *is little more than a paraphrase of Pope's epistles, or yet less than a paraphrase, a mere translation of poetry into prose*.[70] Imperfection, Johnson claimed was a curious idea, for if, as conscious beings, humans can grasp that we are 'more perfect' than unconscious beings, they have no idea that they are less perfect than us. And if we say there is a scale in finite beings, then every finite being on the scale is infinitely below an infinite being, which is what we mean by God.

But it was more about the complacency of Jenyns's views than his faulty logic that Johnson waxed eloquent. 'Poverty,' said Jenyns, 'or the want of riches, is generally compensated by more hopes and less fears.'[71] Johnson, who had known what it was like not to have enough to eat, observed simply, *life must be seen before it can be known*.[72]

Johnson was also caustic about Jenyns's rosy picture of old age, for he may well find *that the imbecillity of old age shall come upon him*.[73] He commented tartly on Jenyns's idea that suffering may be inflicted on us by some higher being. *As we drown whelps and kittens, they amuse themselves now and then with sinking a ship, and stand round the field of Blenheim. . ., as we encircle a cockpit*[74] (at Blenheim in 1704, the English won an overwhelming victory over the French). He could not think for whom some authors – among whom he placed Jenyns – supposed they were writing. *The only end of writing is to enable readers better to enjoy life, or better to endure it.*[75]

Jenyns's system gave nobody pleasure or courage. In the *Free Inquiry*, Johnson discovered the facile arguments of the professing optimists restated with nauseating self-satisfaction. He was angry and pleased that he had savaged Jenyns. *Instead of rising into the light of knowledge we are devolved* [by Jenyns] *back into dark ignorance.*[76]

Jenyns never forgave his reviewer. After Johnson died, Jenyns called his assailant 'A scholar and a Christian – yet a brute'.[77] Johnson was no cosmic Tory, satisfied if the world stayed as it was. His Toryism was rooted in disquieting pessimism. The world could and should be better but probably cannot be. His own sense of dissatisfaction eventually inspired a literary masterpiece.

Johnson had put off visiting his mother. In 1755, he thought of going to see her in Lichfield, but did not. In 1757, John Levett, the man holding the mortgage on the house in Lichfield, was threatening to foreclose and so have grounds for evicting Sarah from her home. Johnson was able to borrow the money that was owed from Tonson, the publisher, thus saving his mother from destitution and himself from shame. Still, he stayed away from Staffordshire.

Finally, in 1759, his stepdaughter Lucy warned him that his mother was dying and he wrote back signing himself to his mother *your dutiful son.*[78] He wrote to her to *say you have been the best mother, and I believe the best woman in the world,*[79] but still he did not move. Foreseeing large bills, he could not borrow any more from Tonson, so he came up with a bright idea.

For a long time, Johnson had revisited, in his imagination, the exotic world about which he had written so many years ago, at the time Tetty lay dying in his translation of the travels of Father Lobo. Two of the *Rambler* essays had involved the story of Seged, Lord of Abyssinia and his quest for happiness. Now that his mother was dying, he was drawn back to the same land.

When Johnson received news that his mother had died, he wrote a serene meditation on death for 'The Idler' on 27 January, and found a group of publishers who would give him £100 for the first edition of his new book, £325 for the second. He calmly discussed the details of his contract and then began to write. He later boasted to Reynolds that he produced his eastern tale in the evenings of a week, which may not have been strictly true, but he did put it together rapidly – it has a sense of fluency that gives the unfolding of the plot a sense of urgency – and on 20 April it was published.

By chance, *The Prince of Abissinia: A Tale* appeared in the same year as Voltaire's *Candide*. Both books, Boswell noted, set out to refute the theory of Optimism, the view that this is the best of all possible worlds. But 'the intention of the writers were very different. Voltaire, I am afraid, meant only by wanton profaneness to obtain a sportive victory over religion and to discredit the belief of a superintending Providence: Johnson meant, by showing the unsatisfactory nature of things temporal to direct the hopes of man to things eternal.'[80]

Voltaire (1694–1778) was the most prominent of the French philosophers, a group of professional writers who acted as critics of received views on religion, ethics and politics. *Candide*, his most famous tale, reads like a farce. Candide, the bastard son of an obscure German baron, is educated by Pangloss, a philosopher, who believes in the theory of Optimism to ludicrous lengths. For much of the time, Candide is looking for his true love, the Baroness Cunegonde and ultimately learns that all theories, not just Optimism, should be discarded. The wise man is content merely to cultivate his garden.

Nobody who has read the two books is likely to deny that Voltaire is much funnier, but the remarks of Boswell have some truth in them. For all his brilliance, Voltaire is confused and confusing, for he hoped to maintain a belief in God while ridiculing the notion of God's ordering of events – such a god would be neither omnipotent nor omniscient, so no God at all.

Meanwhile, Johnson, who was never as entertaining, held a consistent view that as the ways of God are unknowable, human beings who try to comprehend them are presumptuous. He preached the ancient message of the Old Testament wisdom writers or, as one perceptive woman reader put it at the time, the moral of his poem *The Vanity of Human Wishes* was retailed in prose.

An illustration of *The Prince of Abissinia*

Rasselas is the story of Prince Rasselas, fourth son of the Emperor of Abyssinia, who lives fortunately in the happy valley but is not content. He plans to leave it. An engineer offers to enable him to fly but himself has to be rescued from the water. A man of learning, Imlac tells him about his own travels in search of happiness, a story that makes him wish to travel, too. As he is about to escape, he is joined by his sister, Princess Nekayah. With Imlac, they travel to Cairo, where Rasselas visits the city, then a man who cannot practise his own philosophy and a hermit who is only too keen to give up his solitude. Prince and princess separate. While he discovers that men who love public power often lose it, she determines that in private life women left to themselves are trivial and both find out that no marriage is perfect. They visit the Pyramids, where Pekuah, Nekayah's companion, is kidnapped and they must return to the city without her. As her Arab captor was only after money, Pekuah is soon ransomed, having learnt how boring life in a harem is, where no women are capable of being equal to their man. They meet an astronomer who has come to think he controls the heavens. They meet an old man who bemoans age, release the astronomer from his delusions and discuss the value of monastic life. They visit catacombs and wonder why the Egyptians are fascinated by death, a visit that makes Rasselas's desire to work out *to think only on the choice of eternity*.[81] For a while, Rasselas, Nekayah and Pekuah plan how to be happy, while Imlac and the astronomer were *contented to be driven along the stream of life without directing their course to any particular port*.[82] In the end, when the Nile subsides, they agree to go back to Abyssinia.

Nobody reads *Rasselas* for the narrative but the plot lightens the grave discussions that take up most of the book. Johnson showed an unfamiliar, sly sense of humour, as in his comment on the prince's hope to possess a little, well-run kingdom *but he could never fix the limits of his dominion, and was always adding to the number of his subjects*.[83] Johnson suggested men without women grew pompous and that women hidden from men became childish. In most cases, it was better for the sexes to make up for each other's defects. *Marriage has many pains, but celibacy has no pleasures*.[84]

By means of Imlac, he reiterated the view expressed in his critique of Jenyns: *The Europeans... are less unhappy than we, but they are not happy. Human life is everywhere a state in which much is to be endured, and little to be enjoyed*.[85] The view may seem gloomy, but there was a new spring in Johnson's style. He had reason to be content. He was able to defray the costs of his mother's funeral and he went on writing 'The Idler'. He brought the project to a close in April 1760. And in that autumn, King George II died.

A change of life • 1760–1765

Johnson's life was transformed by the death of King George II in October 1760. He was succeeded by his eldest grandson, George III (1738–1820), who was the first Hanoverian to be born and educated in England.

The first two Georges had hated one another, but they shared a devotion to the principality of their birth. Even in the late 1750s, much of England's European diplomacy revolved round the defence of Hanover.

German sympathies made these German kings unpopular in England. Their way of pronouncing English had probably encouraged courtiers to use a long German 'a' and they had something to do with turning Handel, a compatriot, into England's favourite composer, but they had little feel for English concerns.

Their poor grasp of the language hastened the erosion of the King's political power. First Walpole and then the Pelhams had taken over the traditional influence of the Crown. Alone among European sovereigns of powerful countries, they reigned but seldom ruled, and they relied entirely on Whigs, whom Johnson considered a *faction*,[86] to carry on the work of government.

From the beginning, it was obvious that George III was going to be a very different sort of monarch: he was young – just 22 at his accession; he considered himself English; he enjoyed farming; he collected paintings (especially by Gainsborough); and he loved music (especially by Handel). In 1761, he chose as his queen Charlotte of Mecklenburg-Strelitz, a German consort as was

King George III

normal in his family, but unlike his predecessors he loved his wife. Together they had 15 children. (His sons were to be a constant cause of trouble to him and he hated giving his daughters any freedom, so he was not to be a successful father.)

However, in 1761, any failures as a parent lay in the future. What was quickly obvious was that he believed in marriage. His court no longer sported a dreary mistress. His instincts were middle class. He was conscientious, industrious, just religious enough and dull. He also wanted to act like a patriot king.

When he assumed the throne, George III lacked confidence. He could do nothing to stop Parliament from taking control of his finances, but he was determined to make use of his prerogative powers. He knew that he had the right to appoint prime ministers and he, not the Duke of Newcastle, was the source of patronage. He got rid of the elder Pitt, whose ambitious projects he found alarming, and he got rid of Newcastle. He was keen to make peace with Russia, Austria and France – he was a natural Tory and had a Tory distaste for expensive adventures overseas – and he promoted his former tutor, James Stuart (1713–92), to run his government.

In altering the drift of the ministry and in taking back influence, he was probably in tune with the mood of the age. But in promoting his tutor he committed a serious error of judgement, for James Stuart, third Earl of Bute, was a Scotsman. Since 1707, there had been only one Parliament for the whole island of Britain and Scotland maintained a distinct identity in other ways, such as an established Presbyterian church and its own legal system. The unification of the two kingdoms had encouraged Scots to come south to further their careers in a rich country. 'North Britons', as they were called, were caricatured as avaricious, their accents were ridiculed, their loyalty had been suspect, for most Jacobites lived north of the Tweed, while the Black Watch regiment had fought bravely at the siege of Quebec, Highlanders in general remained suspect, the tartan and clan loyalty were proscribed.

To an Englishman who had never been to Scotland and did not want to go there, differences between Highlanders and Lowlanders were rarely understood. John Wilkes (1727–97), a flamboyant journalist, found an easy way to popularity when he set up a weekly paper to ridicule Bute's administration. He called the paper *The North Briton*.

It was from Lord Bute that Johnson heard that the King was minded to award him a pension. The news worried Johnson. He was delighted at the thought that after half a lifetime of scrimping he would be financially secure, but he was worried that the cost of a pension would be the loss of intellectual freedom. In the *Dictionary*, he had defined a *pension* as being *generally understood to mean pay given to a state hireling for treason to his country*.[87] If he were to accept he would be not only a sycophant but also a hypocrite. Not surprisingly, he consulted his friends.

Reynolds, who enjoyed the benefits of well-earned wealth, advised him to accept. He was sure that the pension was a recognition of Johnson's achievement and that the *Dictionary* definition did not apply to Johnson himself. Johnson went away satisfied and did not call on Reynolds until he had called on Bute first. He told Reynolds that Lord Bute had reassured him: *It is not given to you for any thing you are to do, but for what you have done*.[88] However, his enemies were not so kind.

Wilkes's assistant editor was Charles Churchill (1731–64), a dissolute cleric about town. Churchill had already made fun of Johnson as 'Pomposo',[89] a self-important literary hack who had failed to produce the Shakespeare edition for which he had already been paid. Having cruelly laughed at Johnson's physical disabilities, he hit home at his victim's apparent lack of integrity: 'He for his subscribers baits his hook,/ And takes their cash; but where's the book?'[90]

Taking subscriptions was the normal way to underwrite the cost of an expensive book, but so far subscribers had received nothing in return for their money. Indeed, not only had Johnson spent the money, he had also lost the list of names, so that those on whose outlay he depended would not be rewarded by seeing their names within the covers of the masterpiece that they had agreed to fund.

Fortunately, Wilkes and Churchill did not know that, but the award of the pension gave them another grounds for attacking Johnson as a way of getting at Bute. Wilkes sarcastically suggested that in a new edition of the *Dictionary* he should add a footnote explaining that his original definition had been correct for the reign of George II, but in the age of George III the word 'pension' has gained an extra meaning. Now it is 'a reward given to learned men for merit, worth and genius, &c, qualities little regarded at the time this Dictionary was first published'.[91]

Wisely, Johnson kept silent. He did not answer Churchill, treating the man's poetry with contempt. *It had a temporary currency*, he told Boswell, *only from its audacity of abuse*. It would *sink into oblivion*.[92] Wilkes, however, was a more formidable opponent, a rascal of a politician with the gifts of a demagogue. Johnson would go on attacking his opinions and behaviour until Wilkes turned respectable and took to wearing fine lace.

The pension of £300 a year changed Johnson's way of living for ever. In 1758, he had had to leave Gough Square because he could not pay the rent. It was hard to support the members of his ever growing household and for a time he had had to plant

Miss Williams, his old friend from the Birmingham days, in lodgings nearby.

Johnson lived in Fleet Street, then in Inner Temple Lane and always in squalor. In Tetty's lifetime, as she had a drink problem, Johnson had avoided alcohol, but shortly after her death he was drinking again and by 1760 he thought he had a problem, too. He became more indolent, the edition of Shakespeare was laid to one side, he preferred to chat rather than to stand at his desk and work. On Easter Eve, 1761 he wrote down a long list of resolutions: to *repel vain and corrupt imaginations*[93]; to avoid idleness; to regulate his sleeping habits; to plan his days; to keep a diary; to go to Church every Sunday; to read a set part of the Bible every week. He ended by begging God to give him strength to keep to his good intentions. It seems his prayer did not have the desired effect.

In August 1762, just after hearing the good news of his pension, Reynolds invited Johnson to join him on a visit to Devon, Reynolds's home county. It proved to be one of the happiest trips of his life and the forerunner of many more. At Winchester, they called on the scholar Joseph Warton, who was now second master of the College. They had hoped to call on the Earl and Countess of Pembroke – Reynolds had just finished painting the Earl and was in process of painting the Dountess – but his lordship had run away with another woman, and so the two travellers had to content themselves with walking round Wilton House, where Reynolds could admire the superb Van Dycks and Johnson the superb collection of books.

The pair were luckier at Longford Castle, where they stayed the night, and at Kingston Hall, where the host discussed painting and Johnson fell strangely silent. When Boswell's son Sandy called much later on Mr Banks, owner of the Hall, Banks told him that when pointing to a fine detail in one picture, Johnson said, *it is all one to me, light or dark*,[94] whereupon Banks repeated the remark to Reynolds, who replied, 'I can't hear what you say sir.'[95]

A self-portrait by Joshua Reynolds

The blind man and his deaf companion were soon in Devon, where Reynolds's sister Frances wrote an account of Johnson's alarming habits, as when he would make his fingers bend as if he had a cramp, or keep them at chest level as if he were a jockey riding at full speed, or hold them high above his head for a few minutes. His leg movements were even more remarkable, the convulsive movements alarming or arresting.

They moved to a small town called Torrington, where Reynolds had two married sisters. One of his brothers-in-law, William Johnson, went in for increasingly desperate schemes to be rich. His latest idea was to market dried salmon and back in London, Sam would later try to find out if the idea was feasible. Like most of William Johnson's plans, it came to nothing.

In the other household, Sam was more at home. The Palmers lived in a comfortable, elegant house with a garden complete with gazebo, where Johnson retired to read.

Not long after the travellers were in Plymouth, where they stayed for three weeks at the home of one of Reynolds's childhood friends, Dr John Mudge, a man who was to combine being the father of 20 children (by three wives) and a Fellow of the Royal Society. Johnson was impressed with Mudge's scientific erudition but annoyed the current Mrs Mudge by calling her rude when she inquired if he must have an 18th cup of tea.

Johnson was more charming when he and Reynolds visited another house. There, a young lady boasted she could outrun anyone. Commenting, *Madam, you cannot outrun me,*[96] Johnson challenged the young lady to a race. At first she took the lead, as Johnson was wearing slippers too small for him, but when he kicked them off he overtook her. They rejoined the company with the lady on his arm and Johnson smiling with pleasure.

The Johnson who went to Devon was determined to have a good time. But he returned to London in no mood to write; talking was a more pleasant activity and he was good at it. He wondered about his duties as a godfather to one of the Mudge children, as he retained a lively interest in the education of children almost all his life, but he was still unsettled when in May 1763 he met a young man who was to become the most important of all his young friends.

Johnson dropped in on a bookseller, Tom Davies, who was having tea with James Boswell, a Scots gentleman who had just come to town. Boswell was son and heir of a laird, Lord Auchinleck, and desperately anxious to win his father's approval. He had been a Catholic for a month, found that he preferred the pleasures of the town to the monastic life he had imagined for himself, decided against a career in the army in a handsome uniform and was being pressed by his father to study the law. However, Boswell's chief aim was to be loved by the famous. Already he had introduced himself to Garrick, he would introduce himself to Voltaire and Rousseau in a few months time and, though in the end he became one of the greatest of diarists and biographers, at this stage of his life – he was only 22 – he stood out, if at all, as a man with the lightweight instincts of a gossip writer. And yet it is to him that lovers of Johnson are indebted for their picture of the curmudgeon, the man looking for any argument in order to down an opponent, scorning Scots, bluestockings, precocious children, rude, irascible, irregular and repulsive in his personal habits – and yet kindly, like a slobbering bulldog. This Johnson was the artistic construct created by Boswell and the foundation for the edifice was laid, mischievously, by Davies. He told Johnson that Boswell, who was trying to hide his accent, was a Scot. 'Mr Johnson,' said I, 'I do indeed come from Scotland, but I cannot help it.'

That, Sir, I find is what a very great many of your countrymen cannot help.[97]

This first exchange between the future biographer and his subject set the tone for many of their future dialogues. Boswell knew

Johnson only for the last 21 years of Johnson's life. He may have guessed that Johnson would warm to a youngster who enjoyed his company. What neither could have guessed is their exchanges would become classic conversations. Johnson liked people who stood up to him and Boswell's immediate reaction betrayed his nerves but, as the talking continued, Johnson was slowly won over by Boswell's combination of naïve charm and enthusiasm.

Within days, the two were firm friends and, when Boswell left for the continent, Johnson made a point of going to the harbour to see him off. Boswell's friendship with Johnson gave him an entrance into literary London, where men met their friends in clubs, and the raffish and rich spent their evenings in exclusive rooms near Pall Mall, there to drink and gamble their time and their money away. It was not the world of Johnson but that of many of his friends and acquaintances, such as Topham Beauclerk and, later, Charles James Fox (1749–1806). What he valued was the company of intelligent, independent minded men; and his closest friend, Reynolds, understood this well.

In the winter of 1763–64, Reynolds suggested to Johnson that they should found a club of their own. In Reynold's mind, The Literary Club, would have a precise purpose: it would be formed so that Johnson could talk. Among its eight original members were Burke, as yet an unknown politician, and Goldsmith, as yet an unsuccessful writer. Johnson also insisted that Sir John Hawkins must belong. At the same time, he resisted attempts to include Garrick, whom he had known too long. Later he admitted his mistakes. Hawkins proved *unclubable*,[98] a terrible failing so far as he was concerned, and he relented for excluding Garrick.

In the 1770s, Boswell joined, as did Charles James Fox, the Whig politician, Gibbon the historian, Adam Smith (1723–90), the Scots philosopher famous for advocating free trade, Sheridan, the playwright who took to politics, Joseph Banks (1743–1820) the botanist-explorer who voyaged with Cook to the South Seas

James Boswell, Oliver Goldsmith and Samuel Johnson at the Literary Club

and Charles Burney (1726–1814), musicologist father of the novelist Fanny (1752–1840). Many of the cleverest Londoners were glad to be satellites orbiting Johnson. One day, Boswell, with obvious pride, suggested to Johnson that the Club could take over the teaching at St Andrews University and they delightedly discussed which chair would suit which member.

It was Johnson who proposed Boswell's membership in 1773, and it is thanks to Boswell that some of the conversations at the Club have been preserved. Garrick thought that Boswell took notes while his fellow members chatted, but he was wrong. Boswell had trained his memory and, on going home he wrote down what he had heard. He knew Johnson presided at meetings of the Club on Mondays.

Despite Garrick's worries, Boswell has left only one account of an evening at the Club, drawn from the meeting of 3 April 1778. The conversation ranged over the topics of art, emigration, oratory, parliament, the study of languages, travel, judging human behaviour, virtue and temptation, until the members agreed that Johnson must write a letter on their behalf to a gentleman who had offered them a supply of claret when their present stock ran out. It is interesting that, even with Sheridan and Gibbon present, the dominant talkers were Johnson and Burke, but the point is that many had a chance to voice their opinions and all were on their mettle.

In his *Life of Johnson*, Boswell succeeds in conveying to readers the character of his hero and friend. Often, this is done by simply stating what Johnson said. *Sir, a woman's preaching is like a dog's walking on his hind legs. It is not well done; but you are surprised to find it done at all.*[99] Second marriages are *the triumph of hope over experience.*[100] *A man, Sir, should keep his friendship in constant repair.*[101] And for Boswell himself, *Much may be made of a Scotchman, if he be caught young.*[102] Some of the observations are based on prejudice, others on shrewd perception, all are expressed exactly and apt to the circumstances in which they were uttered. Johnson's ability to phrase a thought so precisely and concisely made him hard to defeat in argument.

Johnson, however, was not always out to win – he had heard Boswell was making a collection of information about Scotland. *Make a large book or folio*, he suggested.

Boswell: 'But of what use will it be?'

Johnson: *Never mind the use: do it.*[103]

Johnson did not always play the superior sage, sometimes revealing his own anxieties. Boswell had been to Tyburn (present day Marble Arch) and watched some public executions. He was puzzled that the criminals seemed unperturbed at the prospect of imminent death.

Johnson: *Most of them, Sir, have never thought at all.*

Boswell: 'But is not the fear of death natural to man?'

Johnson: *So much so, Sir, that the whole of life is but keeping away the thoughts of it.*[104]

Johnson went on to say that he was so worried about death that he was not sure whether he wanted a friend to be near him when he was dying or to face God alone. The build-up to the quotable sentences was frequently gradual. *The writer of an epitaph should not be considered as saying nothing but what is strictly true. Allowance must be made for some degree of exaggerated praise. In lapidary inscriptions a man is not upon oath.*[105] It is the last nine words that are remembered, but they have a context and it is the context that gives them their point. The point is all the better because Johnson juxtaposes the ponderous Latinate phrase *lapidary inscriptions* – words cast in stone – with the direct Anglo-Saxon clause *a man is upon oath.*

If it was Boswell's genius to recreate a sense of a man talking, he also conveyed the breadth of Johnson's interests, the warmth of his affections, often for old and insignificant friends who seldom ventured out of Lichfield, and the eccentricity of his behaviour. On one occasion, when staying with Bennet Langton in Lincolnshire, he went up a hill and, announcing that he had not had a good roll for some time, astonished his host by rolling down the hill on his side until he reached the bottom. He was, as he admitted, not over fond of clean linen and when a lady told him he smelled, he corrected her diction by pointing out that, while he stunk, it was she who smelled.

He delighted, irritated and intrigued his friends. Had he just craved male friendship, the Club and the many discussions and debates that Boswell recorded would have satisfied his emotional needs. But what the exclusively male Club could not do was to give him a sense of family and home.

In 1765, Johnson met Hester Thrale, the young, witty wife of Henry Thrale, a rich brewer who asked Johnson to join their households in Streatham and Southwark, with his own rooms. Before 1764, Johnson had often belonged to several dining clubs of some sort. But meeting the Thrales changed his way of life.

A young, intelligent woman with a wide, chaotic education, Mrs Thrale came from a distinguished Welsh family, of which her part had fallen on hard times. Her mother realised this and she let herself be persuaded that she must marry for money. Accordingly, in 1764 the 24-year-old Hester Lynch Salusbury married Henry Thrale, a man 11 or so years her senior, and moved from her beloved hills and mountains to the flat environs of the capital.

Thrale had had a university education but it was his tiny wife who showed a boundless energy for intellectual pursuits. She brought wit and social standing to the marriage; he brought the cash. He had inherited a brewery just south of the river Thames, he had homes in Southwark and in Streatham and he was willing to allow his young wife to became a noted hostess.

So, it was by means of an introduction through Johnson's friend, the dramatist Arthur Murphy (1727–1805), that the Thrales invited the great man to dinner in January 1765, ostensibly for him to meet an acquaintance of Murphy's called James Woodhouse, a shoemaker who had written verses. Before she met Johnson, Murphy was careful to give Mrs Thrale 'generous cautions not to be surprised at his figure, dress or behaviour'.[106] 'We liked one another so well,' she wrote, 'that the next Thursday was appointed for the same company to meet – exclusive of the shoemaker.'[107]

Thus began a friendship that was to last for most of the rest of Johnson's life. Johnson got on well with Thrale. He did not know many businessmen, so he found Thrale's concerns a novelty and in the end his instinctive good sense was of use to a man whom Johnson once described as *rich beyond the dreams of avarice*,[108] but who often took foolish risks.

A detail of Reynolds' portrait of Hester Thrale and her daughter Queenie

In time, the Thrales' connection with Johnson would bring the literary world to Streatham Park. At the beginning of the triangular relationship, however, it was Johnson alone who was at the centre of their lives. As a friend, Johnson was closer to Mrs Thrale than her husband and to Mr Thrale than his wife. The Thrales were never deeply in love; their marriage centred on companionship and their common fondness for Johnson brought them closer together. Johnson and Thrale enjoyed talking of the world, and Johnson was careful to ignore Thrale's philandering.

With Hester, however, there was a deeper bond. She spent many years of her married life pregnant. The birth and upbringing of her children and their frequent deaths in infancy or childhood were the chief occupation of her family life. It was fortunate that Johnson loved children. Luckily for Hester, for all of Johnson's occasional misogyny he also loved intelligent women, and he found in her a gifted linguist, an amusing gossip and a budding poet. In the nursery or the drawing room he was safe.

The year 1764 had contained several important anniversaries: the founding of The Literary Club; the Thrales' wedding; and the bicentenary of Shakespeare's birth.

Between them, Johnson and Garrick did more for Shakespeare's reputation than anyone else in that decade, Garrick as actor-manager and impresario, Johnson as editor. Garrick had first become famous for acting Shakespeare and in 1769, he demonstrated his proprietorial interest in the playwright by staging a Shakespeare festival at Stratford-on-Avon. Boswell thought that when Johnson came to write about Shakespeare, he should admit that Garrick had done a great deal to boost the reputation of Shakespeare. Johnson, however, would have none of it.

Boswell: 'I complained that he had not mentioned Garrick in his *Preface to Shakespeare*.'

David Garrick

Johnson: *Had I mentioned him, I would have had to mention many more.*[109]

Both were right. Johnson was aware that it was not only Garrick who had kept the name of Shakespeare before the theatre-going public but Boswell was also correct that nobody did so much in their generation as Garrick.

There may have been an element of jealousy in this comment, but the great literary achievement that had prompted this discussion makes clear that there was a fundamental difference between Johnson and his former pupil. Garrick was a man of the theatre, whose whole life was dedicated to acting; it was said that he only looked natural on the stage. Johnson, by way of contrast, was a man of the study, who had taken years to become confident enough to express his opinions before the world. Garrick viewed Shakespeare as one playwright concerned with the craft of another. For Johnson, Shakespeare was a poet who had left behind an uncertain text.

It was in 1756 that Johnson had first touted for subscribers for a new edition of Shakespeare. Scholarly labours over many years had prepared him for such a task. In the *Dictionary*, he had quoted Shakespeare more often than any other English writer. His classical training and in particular his study of recent scholarship had made him an exact and penetrating textual scholar. He, too, had tried to write a play, though with only limited success, and he knew the best contemporary dramatists, among them Garrick and Goldsmith. He seems to have started out with some enthusiasm but the distractions of personal problems and other literary projects had delayed his progress in the late 1750s, and for some time after 1760 he did next to nothing. The acquisition of a pension in 1762 freed him from financial worries, enabled him to relax and enjoy long hours of talk with new friends such as Boswell and old ones in the Club.

But there was a further difficulty. The text of Shakespeare was and is hard to determine. In 1616, Shakespeare's eminent rival, Ben Jonson, had seen an edition of his own works through the press and had been careful that even the most ephemeral entertainments such as his court masques would be preserved exactly.

With his plays, however, Shakespeare had been cavalier. Surviving texts are based on actors' memories of them. There is probably no final form of any one of the plays, for as Johnson put it he was *so careless... of future fame*.[110] It is this fact that has given editors so much trouble and so much room for conjecture.

In his *Preface to Shakespeare*, Johnson included a long discussion of his predecessors, which made it clear that he was not surprised that editing Shakespeare had turned into a literary industry. What he might have regretted is that the editing has today become the exclusive concern of Shakespearean experts. Johnson was one of the last who dared to bring his own wide concerns to the business and his annotations are always worth consulting. Commentating on the sentence in *Romeo and Juliet* 'the day is hot', he notes: *in Italy almost all assassinations are committed during the heat of summer.*[111] He pointed out that in Hamlet's 'To be or not to be' soliloquy, the words 'to grunt and sweat', which had become acceptable to modern audiences, were probably incorrect, as *all the old copies* have *to grunt and sweat.*[112]

But sometimes Johnson could just be a pedant. He criticised Shakespeare's image of 'the fiery glow-worm's eyes' in *A Midsummer Night's Dream*: *I know not how Shakespeare, who commonly derived his knowledge of nature from his own observations, happened to place the glow-worm's light in his eyes, which is only in his tail.*[113] Why bother? The mistake showed up Shakespeare's habitual negligence.

When at last Johnson decided that he must write, even though he could not write definitively, he seems to have moved quickly, as was his common practice. The two parts of his edition that have commanded most interest are the noble *Preface* and his comments on the individual plays.

As Johnson was not shy of pointing out Shakespeare's glaring faults, the slovenly plots, the bad jokes, the florid diction, it is worthwhile lingering on his reasons for admiration. He did not react coldly, like a modern professional critic. As a child, he had been terrified by the ghost in *Hamlet*; as an adult he was appalled at the murder of Desdemona in *Othello*. Shakespeare was the dramatist whose plays most reflected human experience: *This is the praise of Shakespeare, that his drama is the mirror of life.*[114] Distinctions between comedy and tragedy did not apply to him, for the one rule Shakespeare followed was to be true to what happens, to the way that people actually behaved, to his own sense of what was common. He may or may not have been well educated. What mattered was *that the greater part of his excellence was the product of his own genius.*[115]

The length and value of Johnson's comments on the individual plays depended on his instinctive reactions to them. He seemed overly earnest when he censured *Twelfth Night* for failing *to produce the proper instruction required in the drama as it exhibits no just picture of life.*[116] He said of *Richard III* that *some parts are trifling, others shocking and some improbable.*[117] He felt obliged to spend a long time explaining why during the reign of James I it was plausible to believe that Macbeth would be tempted by witches. He was perhaps a sounder judge when he dismissed the *fiction*[118] of *Cymbeline* as an example of *unresisting imbecillity*[119] and he anticipated the view of the composer Verdi that the story of *Othello* could have begun as well as ended on the island of Cyprus.

In the *Preface*, Johnson asserted an opinion Garrick would

never have admitted: *A play read, affects the mind like a play acted.*[120] And yet Johnson was not as bookish as other critics, for he was far more open about his feelings than most of the tribe. He found the end of *King Lear* horrific: *I know not if I ever endured to read again the last scenes of the play till I undertook to revise them as an editor.*[121] He had a special reason for being afraid of that play, for in 1765, the year in which the great edition appeared, he was anxious that, like Lear, he would go mad.

At Streatham and in the Club • 1765–1773

For editing Shakespeare, Johnson was awarded a doctorate by Trinity College, Dublin. It was only then that he became entitled to call himself 'Doctor Johnson', as later generations have known him.

At the time, his new dignity may not have offered him much consolation. He had always been prone to melancholia. In the first years of the 1760s, he suffered from all the symptoms of depression. He found it hard to work, to stick to any project, to keep up his spirits. He analysed himself rigorously and, in his opinion, did nothing to remedy the defects he admitted. His mother was dead, the great exploit of the *Dictionary* lay behind him, the flow of his occasional journalism had come to a stop, he stayed in bed late and even his love of talking gave him little pleasure. He had surrounded himself with misfits, and, now that he had a pension, for the first time in six years he could afford to move back into a house. By pure coincidence, the house that he rented at 7 Fleet Street was called Johnson's Court. There, he accommodated his odd group of dependents, who devoted much of their time quarrelling with one another: blind Miss Williams, who

Frank or Francis Barber (1745–1801) was born in Jamaica, and was a slave of the father of Johnson's friend Richard Barber. He was sent to school in Yorkshire, freed and given to Johnson as his servant. Johnson treated him as a son; he and his wife Betsy were living with Johnson in 1784. He retired to Lichfield, got through all the money Johnson left him, then ran a small school until his death.

fancied herself a poetess and was cross that Johnson was slow to find her a printer; the widow Elizabeth Desmoulins, who was a link to the Birmingham past she had shared with Tetty, Johnson's dead wife; Dr Levet, who claimed to be a physician, having once been a waiter in a Parisian café where the clients were medical men; Poll Carmichael, a woman Johnson called *a stupid slut*;[122] and finally, Frank Barber, the former slave and the only person who was young, lively and attractive – he loved women and women loved him, too. Johnson could get away from them only in the huge upper room he used as a study, but he did not want to get away from them for long. He liked chatting at breakfast with Dr Levet and stood by him when he became infatuated with a woman and had assignations with her in a coal shed. Sadly, Mrs Levet, as she became, presented her husband with debts, turned out to be a street walker and was tried for being a pickpocket – by then her husband longed to see her hanged.

Johnson also used his influence to make Miss Williams a published author and wrote a poem himself to pad out her slight collection. He helped Frank when he ran away to join the navy – he wrote to one of the Lords of the Admiralty to get Frank discharged – and he steered him towards marriage.

One day in 1766, the Thrales appeared at Johnson's door. They were worried at the signs of his distress. He no longer came to dine with them once a week. Hester wrote later that he was in the habit of staying in his room for weeks, maybe months at a time. 'When we waited on him one morning,' she wrote, 'and heard him in the most pathetic terms beg the prayers of Dr Delap'[123] – Johnson was on his knees to a clerical friend – she was visibly upset. Meanwhile, her husband, who hated scenes, put his hand over Johnson's mouth to shut him up. Thrale hurried off to work, but not before suggesting to Hester that she should persuade Johnson to come and live with them at Streatham Park for as long as was necessary. Johnson accepted the invitation and stayed for more than three months.

Before Johnson left, he had his own room, as a sort of retreat, and until almost the end of his life he occupied it as a member of the Thrale household. A routine was soon established that was not broken during Thrale's lifetime. Johnson spent weeks with their family and weekends with his own 'family'. As long as this arrangement was in place, there was a shape to his existence.

Hester Thrale was chiefly responsible for Johnson's recovery. He had spent much of his life giving advice. And now that he had found a witty, bright, vivacious woman who was willing to listen to even his most morbid fantasies, he began to relax. Hester was young enough to be his daughter and she mothered him. This was despite her long confinements indoors, preparing for yet another child. Regretfully, she accepted this as a woman's lot and, as she lost so many of her children, she had learned to be resilient. If she felt any distaste for Johnson's distressing and disgusting habits, she hid her feelings. She became the perfect confidante. It is quite likely that Johnson feared he might be carted off to an asylum in a straight jacket; it is clear that he admitted to her his masochistic leanings – he entrusted her with a padlock, apparently to lock him up if he went mad – whatever he said, he felt safe confiding in her. Slowly, her charm soothed him. Like Boswell, she began to record his remarks, such as *life is a pill which none of us can bear to swallow without gilding.*[124] As a wife, she was excluded from the world of affairs, of men's clubs, of life in town. What she provided is an idea of what Johnson was like at home.

Johnson was not always an easy guest. Initially, he annoyed Hester's mother, Mrs Salusbury whose passion for news annoyed him, by inventing events and inserting an account of them into her paper. And her dog annoyed him by eating his buttered toast while he was lecturing her daughter. With time, however, he and the old lady became firm friends and when she died, he wrote her epitaph.

From the start of their relationship, Johnson was able to do much for the Thrales, above all introducing them to his London literary world. The meticulous Reynolds noted a social engagement with the Thrales on 2 September 1766. The eminent painter, soon to become the first President of the Royal Academy and Sir Joshua, was quickly joined by Goldsmith, Edmund Burke, Mrs Burke and Giuseppe Baretti, an Italian man of letters who had settled in London, and was known as 'Joseph' by his English friends. Of these, it was Baretti who became the most familiar face at Streatham, when he was asked to tutor the Thrales' precocious oldest daughter, who was always known by her nickname 'Queenie'. Baretti had first met Johnson in the 1750s, and Johnson helped him with a book explaining Italian for the benefit of those English who were not content to be monolingual.

In 1769, Baretti was fortunate to find that he had eminent and articulate friends. A nervous, excitable man, he was attacked on his way home by a woman and when he defended himself was set upon by three thugs who must have been her accomplices. Being clumsy and short-sighted – the myopia is obvious in Reynolds's portrait of him – he found it impossible to escape and to defend himself he took out a small knife he carried to peel fruit. He struck out wildly and stabbed one of the gang and the man later died of his wounds. The alarmed Baretti gave himself up to the police and they put him in the infamous gaol, Newgate. He was put on trial for murder.

When Baretti's trial occurred on 20 October, he was supported by perhaps the most distinguished group of character witnesses ever to appear together in one relatively insignificant court case. One by one, Burke, Garrick, Beauclerk, Reynolds, Johnson and Goldsmith went into the box to testify. Slowly and loudly, Johnson announced that Baretti was a sober scholar who was by nature peaceable – he did not mention the Italian's fiery temper – but it was the sophisticated men of the world who were of most

Guiseppe 'Joseph' Baretti

use to the defence. Garrick and Beauclerk knew that on the continent, travellers were expected to carry a small knife, as people were offered only forks for a meal. Garrick was questioned: 'When you travel abroad, do you carry such knives as this?'[125] He said yes, explaining that without a knife he could not eat. Baretti was acquitted.

By 1769, Johnson was a celebrity. He had enough vanity to enjoy his new found fame but it had an additional advantage. There was less evidence of frustration for they had been fuelled by a sense of grievance that he was not recognised. With the assurance that he was valued for himself came a new social ease.

A telling example of Johnson's new behaviour is evident in the story of his brief interview with George III. In 1761, the King had bought the London property of the Duke of Buckingham that was on the site of the present Buckingham Palace. There, he kept his library, which Johnson often consulted. When he heard this, George asked to be told when Johnson was present.

One day in February 1767, Frederick Barnard, the librarian, approached Johnson, sitting with a book by the fire, and told him that the King wished to speak to him. Johnson rose to his feet at once and so began a conversation that he remembered with pleasure. The King asked him about the libraries at Oxford, about his own writing, about a controversy over the meaning of the Bible between William Warburton, Bishop of Gloucester, and Robert Lowth, a future Bishop of London – Johnson tactfully said that Warburton had the wider range and Lowth was the sounder scholar – and about John Hill, a fashionable doctor whom Johnson thought a quack. Johnson was about to be snide about Hill, when he thought it unfair to damage the reputation of a man with his sovereign and checked himself. He was delighted that the King told him how much he admired his writing, explained to the King that he had nothing much to say at present but promised that he would listen to the King's request that he write the literary history of the nation.

Johnson told his friends what had happened. One of them, Goldsmith, said that he would have stammered throughout such a dialogue. Goldsmith was also worried. He was anxious in case Johnson would not write him the prologue he had promised for his play, *The Good-natured Man*. Goldsmith should not have worried. In 1768, the play had its first performance, preceded by Johnson's prologue. It may have been true, as Johnson told the King, that he had no great scheme to preoccupy him at the moment, but the absence of any plan to his writing enabled him to respond more easily to the demands of his friends.

Thus, in 1765, after two failed attempts, Henry Thrale offered himself to the electors of Southwark as their prospective MP. He wrote an address that Johnson corrected and, when he had the fortune to be returned unopposed – a frequent occurrence then, as getting elected could be an expensive process – Johnson wrote a letter of thanks to the constituents in the elevated Latinate style of the *Dictionary*. 'I shall think it,' Thrale was made to say, 'the highest happiness to preserve by a constant and uniform attention that concord of which this numerous and opulent Borough has given on this occasion so laudable an example.'[126]

In the election of 1768, however, it seemed likely that more than a few grand words would be needed to ensure Thrale's re-election. London had become a focus of national agitation over the case of Johnson's old nemesis, John Wilkes. Johnson had been lashed by Charles Churchill and Wilkes for accepting a pension from George III. Wilkes's tongue now ran away with him. He had turned from being an idle debauchee as a member of the Hell Fire Club into a formidable demagogue. He may have laughed at Johnson, but he had been much more sarcastic in his strictures on Bute and on the generous terms of peace that Britain offered France in 1763. What's more, if he was anything he was a Whig, and that alone did not endear him to Johnson. But he also convinced Johnson that he had no respect for King or for Parliament. He was MP for Aylesbury when he wrote the 45th number of

his newspaper the *North Briton*, apparently so outrageously critical of the King's speech that in 1764 he was sued for libel. His arrest led to mass protest and the cry of 'Wilkes and Liberty' became the catch phrase of the decade.

Wilkes was quickly released and then, before he could be tried a second time, he fled to Paris and then returned to reclaim his seat in 1768. In these circumstances, the quiet backwaters of Southwark were disturbed by Wilkes mania, especially as he was standing for a seat in Middlesex, not far to the north across the Thames.

A cartoon of John Wilkes holding up the hat of liberty

During the elections, some occupants of carriages were cajoled by riotous mobs into shouting their approval of Wilkes. As Thrale stood by the government, popular agitation might have damaged his chances. His wife helped by laying on dinners for powerful constituents and supporters and in the end, Thrale won easily.

Like him, most of the voters were relatively well-to-do and had no time for Wilkes.

In the midst of the turmoil, Johnson was always ready with encouragement or a fluent pen. The 1768 election did not end the clamour over Wilkes, for when the results for Middlesex were declared he had been elected unopposed. In 1769, on two occasions he was arbitrarily ejected from the House of Commons and re-runs of the election arranged. On the third occasion, there was a government candidate but Wilkes came top of the poll, only for the House of Commons to declare that the man who was a poor second in the vote, a Colonel Lutterell, should take the seat.

'Wilkes and Liberty' now seemed a democratic cause, but not a cause that was favoured at Streatham Park. The clamour stirred Johnson to venture into political pamphleteering in defence of the principles in which he and the Thrales believed. If Hester's recollections are sound, it took him less than two days in 1770 to produce his pamphlet, *The False Alarm*.

In his attitude to established institutions, Johnson was a natural conservative. Since the 'Glorious' Revolution of 1688, it was accepted constitutional theory that ultimate authority in Britain was held by the 'King in Parliament', that is the King and the two Houses of Parliament operating conjointly. It followed that the government had to be acceptable both to the Houses of Parliament and to the King. Because that condition was seldom met in the 1760s, the various ministries of the period were weak. It also followed that it was up to the House of Commons to determine who should be its members. As he was a convicted felon, most MPs believed they were right to exclude Wilkes and Johnson agreed.

Johnson was contemptuous of Wilkes: *Lampoon itself should disdain to speak ill of him of whom no man speaks well.* He was also dismissive of his 'cause': *Every lover of liberty stands doubtful of the fate of posterity, because the chief county in England cannot take its represen-*

tative from a jail. He ridiculed Wilkes's claim that Middlesex is *the chief county*, for it was only since London is within the county's bounds that the county had any importance. Johnson roundly asserted that MPs were *the only judges of their rights.*[129] The electors of Middlesex, he wrote, *either thought* Wilkes *innocent, or were not offended by his guilt.* Johnson was no democrat. He did not believe that 'the people' should decide what is just, while the Wilkites' *original principle* is *the desire of levelling.*[130] He does not deny the conflict of ideas, but he was confident that others would come to see his arguments as sound. All supporters of the existing order in society must do was stand firm. *Nothing . . . is necessary, at this* alarming crisis*, but to consider the alarm as false.*[131] His attack on Wilkes was his favourite political tract. It may have given him a taste for further interventions in the affairs of the day.

In 1770, at last, the King found a congenial prime minister who held sway in the House of Commons. Lord North – the 'Lord' was what is called a courtesy title, for he was oldest son and heir of the Earl of Guildford and as such not yet a peer in his own right – was dedicated to stability. Although, unjustly, he has come to be derided as the man who lost America, (unjustly because the policy of confrontation was the King's) by temperament North hated war. In 1770–71, it seemed that a dispute with Spain might lead to a renewal of conflict just seven years after the Peace of Paris had been signed. To Johnson, as to North, the reasons for the quarrel were trivial.

The ponderous title of Johnson's pamphlet *Thoughts on the Late Transactions respecting Falkland's Islands*, gives a misleading impression of the tone of his vindication of the government's peaceable handling of a delicate situation. His opening sentence presented his moral stance: *to proportion the eagerness of contest to its importance seems too hard a task for human wisdom.*[132] From the start, he implied that it was not worth turning a difference over obscure outposts in the South Seas into a fight. He explained that Britain alone had come to challenge Spain's claim to that part of the Atlantic and he briefly narrated the history of the islands. An Englishman may have been the first naval captain to see them and Frenchmen from St Malo had lingered long enough to name them after their city, and so the name of Las Malvinas was given them by Spain. After Anson had passed by on his way round the world, naval strategists began to assert that they might be important if ever anyone wished to attack *the coasts of Chili* (sic).[133]

If they might be useful in wartime, however, it was hard to see how they would be useful in time of peace, for no occupants could be self-sufficient. Nevertheless, in 1765 a British expedition landed on Falkland's Island – the name then was restricted to the largest island – and a garrison lived there *shrinking from the blast, and shuddering at the billows*.[134] In 1769, a Spanish schooner was sighted and soon settled on another part of the island. In 1770, the governor of Buenos Aires had the British ejected. There were angry discussions between London and Madrid, until the King of Spain disavowed the actions of his governor and the British garrison was restored, yet opposition critics maintained that honour was still not satisfied.

Johnson vehemently repudiated their arguments: *What has been gained? An island thrown aside from human use, stormy in winter, barren in summer . . . which not the southern savages have dignified with habitation*.[135] It is for the titular sovereignty over this place that *a numerous party pretends to wish . . . we had murdered thousands*.[136] Johnson hated war, he had contempt for those who saw it as a glorious activity and he was sure the clamour for war would subside. His predictions proved to be correct. In 1774, while the Spaniards remained at their remote fort, the British evacuated theirs and all ill feeling subsided until after Argentina became independent.

For a devious reason that Johnson did not understand, North ordered that the sales of the pamphlet should be stopped. Probably, Boswell thought, the ministers wished to alter the wording of some passages in their own favour. It did not matter. As Johnson was amused to notice, *a sufficient number were dispersed to do all the mischief, though, perhaps, not to make all the sport that might be expected from it*.[137] Clearly, he was not the sycophant that the government would have liked him to be. What's more, he also put the government's case better than the government itself.

Johnson, of course, had a gift for arguing a case. When Reynolds was made president of the newly founded Royal Academy of Arts, it was said – and it was a topic on which Reynolds was sensitive – that his annual *Discourses* were substantially the work of Johnson. It is likely, however, that all Johnson did was to smarten up Reynolds's prose. Reynolds framed the world as a gentleman painter, rather than as a literary scholar. Thus, when in his first speech he outlined the hope that 'the present age may vie in Arts with that of Leo X and that the dignity of the dying Art (to use an expression of Pliny) may be revived in the age of George the Third',[138] Reynolds tried to imagine what pleasure he would have had to work alongside Leo's favourite artist, Raphael. Except as a name, Raphael meant little to Johnson.

Johnson was delighted to bask in his friend's fame and naturally he was present at the dinner Reynolds laid on to celebrate his own knighthood. He told a friend, *I drank one glass of wine to the health of Sir Joshua Reynolds*.[139] Among those present were Burke and his Catholic father-in-law, Dr Christopher Nugent, Bennet Langton and Robert Chambers (1737–1803), Vinerian professor of Law at Oxford. It was typical of Reynolds that no painter other than himself was there. Equally, it was typical of Johnson that the one person there who was his protégé should be Chambers.

Johnson had always liked the idea of being a lawyer. In 1758, he had recommended Chambers for the Vinerian scholarship and in 1766, Chambers became Vinerian Professor. Chambers's predecessor had been Blackstone, who as author of *The Commentaries* was the most famous jurist in 18th century England. The prospect of a new series of lectures to be drafted and delivered terrified Chambers so he turned to Johnson for help. In the summer, only weeks away the start of the university year, Chambers panicked – he had an acute case of writer's block. His notes were diffuse and he could not think of anything new to say.

Johnson, just recovering from his breakdown, took the coach to Oxford. He was to stay a month. He wrote out a plan of four introductory lectures. He then dictated two-fifths of the first one, to give Chambers a sense of security. That sense did not last. Chambers was humiliated to rely on someone, however famous, who did not have a degree, let alone any training in law. Johnson supplied the structure for the next 16 lectures, on constitutional law but he still had to come back for the second series of lectures, this time on criminal law and Johnson was back with Chambers in February 1768. Sadly, Johnson was ill during this visit to Oxford, but the two of them still put together 14 lectures.

Chambers was eventually knighted when he had became one of the most notable lawyers in the land, but he was always reluctant to publish his first course of lectures. He had no cause for worry, for Johnson said nothing. After his death, Mrs Thrale stated in her *Anecdotes* that 'Innumerable are the prefaces, sermons, lectures, and dedications which he used to make for people who begged of him.'[140]

Boswell, who turned up suddenly in London, in order to enjoy the fame for his book on the history of Corsica (aptly it was a year when the island was in the news, for in 1768 it was ceded by Genoa to France). Johnson was glad to see his young friend again, but beforehand had sent him a letter in Scotland urging him to drop his Corsican obsession.

Boswell was in Oxford for a few days, while Johnson was seeing Chambers, and did not receive the letter until he had returned to London. He protested at once: 'My noble-minded friend, do you not feel for an oppressed nation bravely struggling to be

A portrait of the young James Boswell

free? . . . Empty my head of Corsica! Empty it of honour, empty it of humanity, empty it of friendship, empty it of piety.'[141]

When Johnson came back to town, he accepted Boswell's rebuke with a good grace. But he also continued pontificating on the cant preached by those who spoke in favour of political liberty – it was becoming one of his obsessions.

In this year, Boswell first met Hester Thrale, when she came in her coach to collect Johnson from Johnson's Court. In fact, he leapt on to the coach, so that Johnson had to introduce him. Boswell took care to relay that he was 'as Johnsonian as herself'[142] – he regarded Johnson as a great find and he wished to be sure that no one else had more right to Johnson than he did. It was a battle that it would take years to win.

In one respect, Boswell is a better witness than Mrs Thrale, for he belonged to the all-male world in which Johnson passed much of his time. He invited Johnson to dinner with friends who included Reynolds, Garrick and Goldsmith and listened to them discussing the relative merits of Dryden, Pope and Shakespeare. He noticed how Garrick and Johnson teased one another, until matters became serious when Johnson said that there were lines in Pope better than anything in Shakespeare. Boswell had a knack of getting himself invited by those whom he wanted to meet and so he had tea with Miss Williams, a sign of special recognition. He asked Johnson how he would rear a child. Johnson replied he would wash it in warm water. *No, Sir, the hardy method of treating children does no good*.[143]

It was an even greater honour to be asked to dine on Easter day and so, after a morning in St Paul's Cathedral, Boswell walked to Fleet Street. Boswell twitted him: 'What is the reason that women servants . . . have much lower wages than men servants . . . when . . . our female house servants work much harder than the male?' Johnson had no answer. At another meal Johnson judged a woman more harshly than a man who had been as guilty as she was.

Among male friends, Johnson had a predilection for attractive rakes. Before meeting Boswell, he enjoyed the company of the charming Topham Beauclerk. This did not mean that he approved of Beauclerk. Beauclerk was cited in a divorce case and married the woman he had seduced but when Boswell tried to defend her for leaving her first husband, Johnson commented *the woman's a whore, and there's an end on it.*[144]

Through his journals, Boswell has become better known than Johnson. The image of himself that Boswell reveals in the journals makes his friendship with Johnson all the more intriguing, for he behaved like a rake, too. He told Johnson he was making notes and Johnson knew it. He also trained his memory. The marvellous dialogues that he recorded were to be the main source of the later *Life*.

Boswell did not know all that was central to Johnson's life. In 1773, Boswell thought he had joined the inner circle when Johnson made sure that he became a member of the Club. He could not have known that in the same year, Johnson wrote a letter to Hester Thrale in French asking her to keep a padlock, so that if need be she could confine him until she decided he was fit to be let out. He was so afraid of going mad that he wanted to ensure he would not be locked up in a mental hospital.

There was a dark side to Johnson's relationship with her of which Boswell was unaware. Had he known it, he might have been shocked, for Boswell needed to have a hero and in Johnson he thought he had found one. Hester was wiser. She realised that nothing was better for Johnson than her habit of immersing him in the everyday life of a family. The Thrales made him feel at home.

In any case, in 1772 and 1773 the Thrales found they had to cope with serious troubles of their own. Thrale was too restless a man to be content merely to be rich and he had overreached himself just when a bank in London went bankrupt. Suddenly, he had no capital on which to draw. Luckily, Johnson and Hester were at hand. Johnson calmed him with good advice. Hester, though pregnant, drove to Brighton to organise a loan of £5,000 from a family friend and she borrowed from her own family. The firm was saved, but she lost her baby ten hours after its birth.

The following year was almost worse. Henry Thrale's casual extramarital affairs were mentioned by a gossip columnist in the section of a paper called the 'Court of Cupid'. Already humiliated by his failures as a businessman, Thrale was next attacked over Johnson's presence in his home and it was implied that young Henry, Thrale's son, looked like the author who was his guest. For some while, Johnson had kept his distance but when he expressed worry about the state of his eyes, Hester brought him back to Streatham where he found his former antagonist, Hester's mother, was dying. Thrale was cheered up when the Prime Minister, Lord North, now Chancellor of Oxford University, arranged an honorary doctorate for him. Johnson may have felt a little redundant. He began to think of taking up Boswell's suggestion that the two of them should explore the wilds of Scotland.

The delights of travel • 1773–1777

The man who is tired of London is tired of life,[145] said Johnson and yet for much of his career he had expressed a fascination with foreign parts. As a young man, he had translated and written an introduction to a Portuguese missionary's account of Abyssinia and as a mature man he had set his philosophical tale *Rasselas* there and in Egypt.

For the armchair traveller that he was, there was no better place to be than in London. Merchants in the City needed to know the price of commodities worldwide, the Society for the Propagation of the Gospel sought out information about the new peoples to evangelise and, confident of technological superiority over all rivals that were not European, adventurous sailors set out to explore the vast spaces and unknown coastlines of the Pacific Ocean. Their tales were eagerly listened to by a public that seemed insatiable in its desire to hear about distant places.

As he entered his mid-60s, Johnson's curiosity remained boundless and it was his good fortune that in the 1770s he had the chance to learn much more. What he probably did not expect was that he would be learning it through first-hand experience.

In terms of global exploration, the decade was as exciting a period as that after Columbus first crossed the Atlantic. Among the new explorers, the most remarkable, as a navigator, was Captain James Cook (1728–79). Though the French settled in Tahiti, thanks to him the English made the greatest gains in the Pacific, when his careful searches made his countrymen aware of New Zealand and Australia.

Cook came back from his first voyage in 1775 and Boswell made it his business to meet the new hero. He told Johnson that after talking to Cook he 'felt a strong inclination to go with him on his next voyage.'[146]

Both Boswell and Johnson were sceptical about some of the observations made by the geographers, for without knowledge of languages how could anyone understand the politics, morality and religion of an area? The naturalists had fewer problems. The French had established a habit of sending astronomers and botanists along with the sailors and Cook, though not a professional scientist himself, was entrusted on his very first voyage with observing the transit of Venus in the southern hemisphere.

The man who captivated London society with his anecdotes of the South Seas was Joseph Banks. His standing was due in part to his social position – he had been educated at Eton – and in part to his skill as an observer – he became President of the Royal Society. Banks was elected a member of the Club in 1778 and he told Johnson about kangaroos. On one occasion, Johnson astonished a group of men by demonstrating what a kangaroo looked like and how it moved. 'He stood erect,' wrote Boswell, 'put out his hands like feelers, and, gathering up the tails of his huge brown coat so as to resemble the pouch of the animal, made two or three vigorous bounds across the room.'[147]

He was even more intrigued by another of Banks's finds: a Polynesian prince called Omai (fl.1774–76). Omai was a handsome fellow and Reynolds made him the subject of a magnificent picture, standing in the pose of the *Apollo Belvedere* – a pose he had used long ago for his friend Keppel – displaying the tattooed hands typical of his nation and dressed in a long white robe and turban that looked as much Turkish as Tahitian. In Omai, society ladies who admired a fine body thought they had found the noble savage of their dreams.

Johnson, however, would have none of it. He had met Omai

and was taken by the *elegance of his behaviour. Sir*, he told Boswell, *he has passed his time in England, only in the best company; so that all he had acquired of our manners was genteel.*[148] What neither of them knew was that Omai was making friends in London so he would be armed with European weapons when he carried out his plan to take revenge on enemies back home.

It was Boswell who first persuaded Johnson to travel, and the kangaroo incident occurred during Johnson's own great adventure. Despite ill health and his love of Streatham Park, Johnson allowed himself to be persuaded by Boswell to journey through the Highlands and to the western isles. Boswell wished to force the professional anti-Scot to venture into Scotland, and he looked forward to setting up the kinds of meetings that were his speciality, such as an encounter between his austere, Presbyterian, Whig father with his convivial, Anglican, Tory adopted father figure (oddly he took no notes of the encounter). Boswell also wanted to see Johnson react to the simple ways of an impoverished people. They were on the road from August to November 1773.

A cartoon of Johnson on his walking tour of the Highlands

In that year, the more remote areas of Scotland were not imbued with the fake Victorian sentimentality that lends glamour to hairy men in kilts dancing on swords, tossing cabers, eating haggis and downing a dram or two of whisky. Scotland was a poor country that had been subjected by its richer neighbour. The English had some respect for the Lowlanders who lived in the south and the east of the land, but then Lowlanders had accepted that there were advantages for them in the English connection. While in 1707 they had lost their parliament in Edinburgh, they had kept their law and their Kirk, the Presbyterian church, as national institutions. While England had only two universities at Oxford and Cambridge, Scotland could boast four, at Edinburgh, Glasgow, St Andrew's and Aberdeen, respectively, and to each of them Johnson paid a visit. He loathed to admit that a Presbyterian cleric was in any way as learned as an erudite Anglican, but when he talked to university men in Scotland he was, as it were, almost on his own territory. Many of them shared his veneration for the neo-Latin writers of the 16th and 17th centuries, among whom George Buchanan (1506–82) was a leading light and the man responsible for making James VI (VI of Scotland, I of England) a prize school-boy rather than an intelligent monarch.

In terms of modern learning, Scotland was enjoying an age of enlightenment. If Hume, the philosopher and historian, was an international figure whose atheism meant Johnson considered him almost as wicked as three Frenchmen, Voltaire, Diderot and Rousseau, then he met and often came to know well others who were eminent on any scale of reputation: Adam Smith (1723–90), moral theorist and economist; William Robertson (1721–93), historian; James Beattie (1735–1803), philosopher and poet; Alexander Wedderburn (1733–1805) lawyer; Lord Monboddo (1714–99), archaeologist before the subject became a science.

Among such people, Johnson was in his element. But he had not come north to discuss topics he could discuss in London and with men who, like Smith, had anticipated his advice by coming south: *The noblest prospect which a Scotchman ever sees, is the high road that leads him to England.*[149] Johnson was impatient to meet people he was unlikely to come across, to find common humanity in those with whom, superficially, he had little in common. His road would take him into the mountains and glens beyond the Highland Line and to the tiny islands that lay off the western coast.

At Nairn, he noted, *we may fix the verge of the Highlands; for here I first saw peat fires, and first heard the Erse* (or Gaelic) *language.*[150] He called Inverness, which lay a little way further along the coast, *the last place which had a regular communication by high roads with the southern counties.*[151] He enjoyed reminders of the story of Macbeth: Fores, the town to which Macbeth was travelling when he came across the witches; Calder or Cawdor castle, of which he became thane; and castle ruins at Inverness, *said to be the castle of Macbeth.*[152] But he seldom showed much Romantic attachment to relics of the past. He was, as he put it, a student of manners; he wished to understand the highlanders and islanders, and he was keenly aware that since 1745, their ancient way of life had been discarded. The clan system was disrupted, clansmen disarmed, the wearing of the tartan plaid was proscribed, English troops garrisoned the major towns and English roads had opened up routes inland. If Scots did not emigrate south, many of them already were setting out on what would become a series of national trails to Canada, America, Australia and New Zealand. Their native soil was poor and barren, often treeless, and life was hard.

Johnson was sufficiently unpretentious to be touched by the many examples of hospitality he encountered. At the first Highland hut he saw, on the side of Loch Ness, he experienced *the old laws of hospitality*[153] that allowed a stranger to enter uninvited and the old woman who owned the hut promptly offered Johnson and Boswell some whisky.

Johnson was more surprised at Anoch, where *a young lady not inelegant either in mien* (appearance) *or dress*[154] asked them if they would like tea. Johnson was so delighted that he gave her the book he had and later commented that *he would not be pleased to think that she forgets me.*[155]

Soon, as they made for the coast, he could reflect that he found himself in a deserted landscape. *Yet what are those hillocks to the ridges of Taurus* (the mountain ranges of eastern Turkey) *or these spots of wildness to the deserts of America?*[156]

On 1 September, as they neared the coast, Johnson was in a more belligerent mood. After climbing up and down the mountain called the Rattakin (Rattachan), Boswell rode on ahead and Johnson was furious with him. Luckily, the next day he forgave his companion and in the rain together they crossed the sea to Skye.

Moving to the isles brought the two of them closer human contacts. The first man they tried to imbue with enthusiasm for 'feudal and patriarchal feelings',[157] as Boswell put it, proved more realistic than them, for their host, Sir Alexander Macdonald, had been a scholar at Eton. Johnson said he would make Skye an independent island. *Sir, I would have a magazine of arms.* Sir Alexander replied laconically, 'They would rust.'[158]

A week later, they crossed a choppy stretch of water to Raasay and Johnson's spurs fell overboard. He coped with misadventure by discussing a favourite topic – the authenticity of the so-called poems of Ossian that had been published (in fact, fabricated) by the contemporary writer James Macpherson – and by listening intently to the genuine Erse songs that the rowers chanted.

A bevy of Macleods, headed by the laird of the island himself, met them on the shore. They reached Raasay's home just in time to drink a dram of brandy at six o'clock before a fiddler arrived and the company danced, much to Johnson's delight. The next day it rained and Johnson ventured out only on a short expedition to look at an old chapel. Boswell went out shooting after dinner with a new friend, Malcolm Macleod, and returned to find Johnson musing on the fact that one of the party, the Laird of Mackinnon, had been misled by Hume's arguments against miracles. He had studied himself into infidelity, explained Boswell. *Then he must study himself out of it again. That is the way. Drinking largely will sober him again.*[159]

They returned to Skye and it was there that Boswell witnessed one of those encounters that he had a genius for observing. 'To see Dr Samuel Johnson, the great champion of the English Tories, salute Miss Flora Macdonald (1722–90) in the isle of Skye, was a striking sight; for though somewhat congenial in their notions, it was very improbable they should meet here.'[160] Flora Macdonald was, in fact, a married woman and the mistress of Kingsburgh, where they were her guests. But when Boswell made his journal public, he knew that his readers would always think of her as the lady who had saved Bonnie Prince Charlie from his Hanoverian pursuers.

In his Journey, Johnson called Flora Macdonald a woman of middle stature, soft features, gentle manners, and elegant presence.[161] Boswell preferred to retell the whole story of her adventures with the Jacobite heir. After an overwhelming defeat at Culloden, the fugitive prince had made his way to the west to take a ship back to France and Macdonald had helped him evade capture by dressing him up as her maid.

Johnson questioned her indirectly – he never suggested that he knew who she was – about her adventures with 'the Wanderer' as his supporters had called the Stuart Prince, and Boswell recorded her detailed reply. He was proud that his new friend Malcolm Macleod had also been involved. Malcolm had been open about his support of the Jacobite cause but the government could not find enough witnesses to accuse him. He was taken to London to be tried, only to find himself released and, when Flora Macdonald was released too and asked whom she would like to escort her home, she chose him. 'I went to London to be hanged,' he told Boswell, 'and returned in a post-chaise with Miss Flora Macdonald.'[162]

The stay on Skye was notable as an opportunity for the two to indulge their Jacobite sympathies, but in human terms perhaps no person they met on their travels came to matter to them so much as Donald Maclean, the young Laird of Col, whom Boswell approached with a letter from Professor MacLeod of Aberdeen, the young Col's uncle. He met them on 25 September and stayed with them until 19 October. A small, neatly dressed man, he had the best of intentions for his tenants. He had studied farming in Hertfordshire and Herefordshire and wished to make agriculture profitable on his own lands without oppressing those who worked for him. Johnson became a keen admirer. *He is a noble animal. He is as complete an islander as the mind can figure. He is a farmer, a sailor, a hunter, a fisher: he will run you down a dog: if any man has tail, it is Col.*[163]

A man with 'tail' was one who happily combined animal with rational qualities. He regretted that Col was not quite intellectual enough, yet pleased that Col was prepared to disagree with him – he could not abide people who would not stand up to him.

Col knew that they wished to go to Iona, but he proposed a much wider circuit though the isles, to include Mull, Eigg, Muck, Coll and Tiree. Col, as Boswell put it, was now their leader. For some days, winds and rain delayed their plans, until at last Col and his servant suggested that in spite of the rough weather they might make for one of the harbours on Coll itself, the isle that gave him his title. The decision was taken when they were already well out to sea in a small cargo boat that was being buffeted by the waves and, had the skipper of the boat made even the slightest mistake, they could have been dashed on the rocks. While the boat pitched and rolled, Boswell clung to a rope that he later saw was of use only to keep him on board, for it was attached to a masthead. Johnson, meanwhile, unaware of the danger they were in, slept peacefully with one of Col's greyhounds at his back. Eventually, Col cried out, 'Thank God we are safe!'[164] and they cast anchor in the bay.

They had to endure more autumn storms before Col got them on shore at Mull. As they were about to say good-bye to him, Johnson commented, *Col does everything for us: we will erect a statue to Col.*[165] They provided him with lasting memorials in the eloquent accounts of the young man that can be read in Johnson's *Journey* and Boswell's *Journal*, but in his beloved isles he was soon forgotten. The following year, he drowned.

And so they came to Iona, from where Columba preached the gospel to the Scots. It was Johnson who found words appropriate to the place. *We were now treading that illustrious island, which was once the luminary of the Caledonian regions, whence savage clans and roving barbarians derived the benefits of knowledge and the blessings of religion . . . That man is little to be envied, . . . whose piety would not grow warmer among the ruins of Iona.*[166]

Johnson takes a rest on his Highland tour

Three days later they were sleeping at Oban. They were back on the mainland and relieved to know that they were no longer at the mercy of tides and currents and they could be anywhere they wanted to be in Scotland or England in a matter of days. Johnson marked their new security by downing his first gill of whisky, leaving only a drop for Boswell. They were now drinking companions and a fortnight later, Johnson took the high road to England.

Scotland had been an experience like no other in his life. Adventures north of the border provided Johnson with the excuse to try his hand at a new kind of writing: travel writing. His *Journey to the Western Isles of Scotland* was rushed into print in 1775.

Since 1785, when Boswell's *Journal of a Tour to the Hebrides* appeared, Boswell has been judged, correctly, to be more entertaining, and his style is more modern and indiscreet. But the aims of Johnson were different. He was not obsessed with the need for a good story but he wished to understand people that were remote from the world he knew. He was intrigued by their habits, the way they walked in shoes called brogues, the playing of the bagpipe (which he liked), their food – he came to value a Scots breakfast – and the economic and social problems that beset them in the years after the collapse of the clan system in 1745–46. He still made jokes about the Scots, but he had learned to love many of them. He ended his account on a note of humility alien to the bumptious Boswell. *Having passed my time almost wholly in cities, I may have been surprised by modes of life and appearance of nature, that are familiar to men of wider and more varied conversation. Novelty and ignorance must always be reciprocal, and I cannot but be conscious that my thoughts on national manners, are the thoughts of one who has seen but little.*[167]

No other expedition Johnson went on moved him so much as his journey to the western isles. But having got the taste for travel he was delighted to enjoy a new passion.

In 1774, prosperity had returned to the Thrale household and Hester and Johnson started to discuss some long tour together. They both wanted to go abroad and were attracted by the idea of a long journey to Rome to see the antiquities. After all, many rich English men and women regarded a stay in Rome as an essential part of one's education, a view held by Reynolds, Johnson's best friend.

However, Henry Thrale vetoed the idea because he thought Hester should go to north Wales to see the state of her property there. And so, in July the Thrales, Queenie and Johnson set out, via Lichfield, for her ancestral lands.

Hester was proud to show off the place where she was born,

near Pwllheli but, though Thrale enjoyed the fine views, the near-sighted Johnson kept his nose in books, and neither shared her enthusiasm. On the way back they called in at Hagley, site of one of the most beautiful parks in England, but were coolly received by the owners. On another social call, this time on the Burke household in Beaconsfield, they were put out by their host's heavy drinking. Hester, however, was undeterred and, having been lent Boswell's rough draft of his Highland journal, she became ambitious to undertake a more exciting tour.

In September 1775, the same party that had gone to Wales set out for Paris, with the useful addition of Baretti, their common friend, who had fluent French. Hester and Johnson could both read the language, but neither had ever heard it. She would try anything and would use scraps of English, French, Latin and Italian in order to make herself understood. Johnson, however, would not stoop to pronouncing French badly, so he took refuge in Latin. In Rouen, he enjoyed a long discussion with an interesting abbé on the destruction of the Jesuits. On 22 October, he told Dr Levet what he had been doing: *We came yesterday from Fontainebleau, where the court is now. We went to see the King and Queen at dinner, and the Queen was so impressed with Miss* (Queenie), *that she sent one of the gentlemen to inquire who she was . . . Mrs Thrale got into a convent of nuns . . . and I am very kindly used by the English Benedictine friars.*[168] The 'friars' were, in fact, monks of the monastery of St Edward's. During the revolution they would move to Douai and a century later they came back to England.

Whatever anti-Catholic prejudices he felt, Johnson was at ease with them. They, like the abbé and himself, belonged to one large, international, Latin-speaking community. He enjoyed Paris, but he told Boswell, *Paris is, indeed, a place very different from the Hebrides, but it is to a hasty traveller not so fertile of novelty, nor affords so many opportunities of remark.*[169]

When the party returned to London, they talked of making

the postponed trip to Italy, only to find that a Thrale family tragedy ruled out any such jaunt. In early 1776, Hester's favourite child, Henry, her only living son, fell ill and within hours was dead of a ruptured appendix. Johnson, who had been in Lichfield, hurried back to comfort her and in place of the planned Italian tour, Hester went to Bath to recover.

During the mid-1770s, Johnson's chief intellectual concern was modern politics. In 1774, there was another election in Southwark and, as usual, many supporters of Wilkes rioted. Once again, the exclusive British franchise enabled a few voters to send Henry Thrale back to parliament as one of the constituency's MPs.

Johnson signalled his belief in his friend and his distaste for those he thought of as the mob by dashing off a pamphlet called *The Patriot*. Wilkites considered themselves patriotic, a claim that Johnson ridiculed, for he thought their patriotism *a species of disease*[170] as they were bent on stirring up discontent. But his targets were not just local ones, for the great debate of the age involved Britain's relations with its mainland American colonies. *That man is no patriot, who justifies the ridiculous claims of American usurpation; who endeavours to deprive the nation of its natural and lawful authority over its colonies.*[171] On this issue, he was at one with his King. Colonists who denied the Crown's authority had no good case.

No taxation without representation was the rallying cry of the American patriots who claimed that the British parliament had no right to order the levying of taxes on them as they sent no MPs to Westminster. The slogan seems to have originated in 1765, when a national Congress met to discuss how to resist the Stamp Act that had been imposed on all legal documents in America to help pay for the nine-year-long French and Indian war of 1745–63.

The last and most famous of his political pamphlets was a direct attack on the slogan used by Americans to justify repudiating the taxes that the British Parliament had imposed on them: 'No taxation without representation.'

Always bold, Johnson chose a provocative title: *Taxation no tyranny*. His assumptions were colonialist, in that he correctly maintained that all other European rulers claimed the right to lay down laws for their colonial subjects. The British had borne the expense of protecting the Americans in wartime; now they were within their rights in asking Americans to bear some of that financial burden in peacetime. If Americans *had a right to English privileges, they were accountable to English laws.*[172]

Just as he had argued against Wilkites, he also believed that the existing state of things was the best. He would not concede that some changes might be good – he did not even hold with the view that his friend Burke would put forward against the French revolutionary radicals, that gradual change was good – and so his Toryism could make no concessions to Americans on the verge of rebellion. In previous conflicts, such as the Falkland Islands, he had put forward arguments in favour of keeping the peace. Now, he saw no way of making concessions that would be acceptable to the radical colonists. However, his hatred of hypocrisy led him to make one shrewd hit at the American patriotic case. *How is it that we hear the loudest yelps for liberty among the drivers of negroes?*[173]

Johnson hated the institution of slavery and he knew that almost none of the American leaders attacked it. As so often with Johnson, his heart was more enlightened than his mind. From a distant viewpoint it is hard to see how England, thousands of miles from its colonies, could continue to run them without making many accommodations with the colonial ruling class, whether the gentlemen plantation-owners of Virginia or the merchants of Boston and New York. Johnson may have been wrong-headed in his attachment to existing constitutional arrangements but his position on social and moral matters can seem surprisingly modern.

Slavery was just one issue on which Johnson held unconventional opinions. He also wanted to reduce the incidence of capital punishment and in 1777, he was invited to intervene in a celebrated case.

Dr Dodd (1729–77) was a well-known clergyman whom Johnson scarcely knew, a fashionable preacher and one-time royal chaplain. Like Johnson, he disapproved of slavery. Unlike Johnson, he found it hard to control expenditure and it was this that led to disaster. He had once been tutor to the fifth Earl of Chesterfield, heir of Johnson's

America was the political issue of the 1770s. To the modern reader, Johnson must seem a reactionary but no European colony had revolted before and the modern dislike of 'colonialism' would have been incomprehensible.

In fact, Johnson distrusted the motives of the colonisers. What many Americans hated most about British policy was the Quebec Act (1774), which restricted their ability to colonise lands to which the French-Canadians of Quebec laid claim. In that sense, the Virginians who wished to absorb land to the west were more colonialist than the British.

hated 'patron', and he assumed that his lordship would not mind if he 'borrowed' a little money, which he did by forging a cheque – he was sure he would be able to repay what he owed. What he had not calculated was that his former pupil would object. Chesterfield took him to court and Dodd was convicted of forgery, which was a capital crime.

It was then that Dodd remembered he had met Johnson and through the Countess of Harrington he appealed for his help. *I will do what I can*,[174] was Johnson's immediate reaction, and almost at once he began on an extraordinary one-man campaign on behalf of Dodd.

Johnson wrote a speech for Dodd to be delivered before the Recorder of London at the Old Bailey, when he was about to be sentenced to death. He drafted a sermon, *The Convict's Address to his Unhappy Brethren* for Dodd to preach, with his own additions, in Newgate prison chapel. He wrote a series of letters to eminent men, including Lord Chancellor Bathurst, Lord Chief Justice Mansfield, the most famous lawyer in the country – and a petition from Mrs Dodd to the Queen. He wrote a newspaper article when Earl Percy organised a petition on Dodd's behalf, he submitted a petition to be sent from the City of London, which the City chose to alter, and finally he wrote an appeal to the King. *May it not offend your Majesty, that the most miserable of men applies himself to your clemency, as his last hope and his last refuge; that your mercy is most earnestly and humbly implored by a clergyman, whom your laws and judges have condemned to the horror and ignominy of a public execution.*[175] As far as Johnson was concerned, Dodd's great anxiety was that he had not had time to repent of his numerous sins. The appeal failed and, as he prepared for his end, Dodd wrote to thank Johnson for being his 'comforter', his 'advocate' and his 'friend'.[176]

On 26 June 1777, Johnson wrote back to reassure Dodd: *And may God . . . who desireth not our death, accept your repentance . . . let me beg that you make in your devotions one petition for my eternal welfare.*[177] On a copy of this letter, Boswell found that Johnson had written one comment: *Next day, June 27, he was executed.*[178]

The mid-1770s proved to be an exciting time for Johnson. He had acquired a wider understanding of Britain by his visits to the Highlands and islands of Scotland and the hills of North Wales, and he had seen the court and capital of Britain's most persistent rival on the continent. He had actively supported the Tory principles that he believed answered the objections of those who demonstrated for 'Wilkes and Liberty' at home or, in America, upheld the right of rebellion against the so-called tyrant, King George III. His writing placed him at the centre of national life. He had achieved a status that few professional writers have ever occupied in English national life – the one obviously comparable figure must be Dickens – and this meant that his voice was heard, even on a contentious matter such as a sentence of capital punishment. By 1777, many people wanted to know: what does Doctor Johnson think? In that year he was asked to pronounce his verdicts on modern English poets.

Among the poets • 1777–1784

In 1767, King George III had suggested to Johnson that he should write a literary history of England. Johnson had listened to his monarch's words respectfully, but he had probably never thought about the idea again until he was approached by a group of publishers with a request to put something like the royal idea into practice.

Johnson was invited to write prefaces for a collection of English poets. The poets were to be modern poets – even Johnson would have baulked at a book that went back to the age of Chaucer, let alone that of *Beowulf* – and so it would be a more up-to-date work that the sort of anthology made up of works quoted in the *Dictionary*. There, he had placed the late Elizabethan age at the start of the development of modern English. And yet he and his publishers knew that there was another divide in the story of modern taste.

The restoration of Charles II in 1660 had coincided with the birth of modern literature. The theatres that opened in Covent Garden and Drury Lane were not like Shakespeare's Globe Theatre with its stage open to the elements, or even the more intimate theatres in grand halls. The new theatres made use of the proscenium arch to divide the spectators from the actors – or most of them, for, until Garrick stopped the habit, the nobility sometimes took seats on the stage. The tragedies that were enacted set their subjects in exotic lands such as Mexico or India, where speakers took naturally to the new fashion for speaking in rhyming

A lithograph of Dr Johnson studying entries into the dictionary

couplets. Comedies took place in modern England, where the court set an easy standard in marriage morals. Ease of manner became the style demanded by gentlemen and ladies and literary essays by Dryden and philosophical essays by Locke aimed to win over readers by use of a throw-away tone. Had Johnson been able to read Pepys (who could not be read until the early 19th century, when the code he used had been cracked), he would have found that his diaries cultivated a fresh directness. At the same time, scientists in the Royal Society tried to make the English language clearer. Inevitably, the poetry that appeared in print was meant to be up-to-date in a new way.

London acquired the coffee houses that Johnson took for granted and, as this was the period when the London season was established, women of a certain social class were aware of the latest fashions in ways women of previous generations could not have conceived. The steady march of women to the front of the reading classes had begun. With the introduction of the novel in the early 18th century, feminine influence on the writers who meant to be popular became pronounced. Johnson's friend Samuel Richardson, author of *Pamela* and *Clarissa*, wrote for women and surrounded himself with women admirers. Male poets slowly began to realise that they must write for women, too and men became men with sentimental emotions, or as they put it then, with sensibility. Thus, in 1771, Henry Mackenzie published a novel called *The Man of Feeling*.

Johnson was no mere scholar lost in the past. He may have felt at home with a Latin or neo-Latin text in his hand, but he was not an obscure scholar lost in veneration of past literary glories. For years, he had tried to keep abreast of recent writing. He knew many lines of modern poetry by heart. He had met several of the poets. He was used to discussing the latest literary fads. Now, he was given a final opportunity to record his view of modern literature for his own and all future ages.

The contract he signed with 36 booksellers, who were careful to deal with him through old friends of his, Tom Davies, William Strahan and Thomas Cadell, who had shared in the publication of his *Journey to the Western Islands*, was intended to respond to a similar venture undertaken by an Edinburgh firm; the London book traders would not let the Scots take over English poetry. They had decided about whom Johnson should write and, though to friends he grumbled that he did not have charge of the operation, he insisted that certain names should be added to the list: one major poet, James Thomson; and four minor ones, whom Johnson thought were just as good as any of the minor poets already chosen for him. Of these, the only familiar author is Isaac Watts, who may be ranked with Charles Wesley or William Cowper among 18th century hymn writers. 'When I survey the wondrous cross' and 'Oh (his word was 'Our') God, our help in ages past'[179] have lasted and enduring fame is one of Johnson's tests of poetry's abiding worth. What is strange, considering his insistence that he wrote only for money, is that he suggested to the publishers a payment of 200 guineas. In the end, they gave him £100 more – Johnson needed the stimulus of being asked to write.

Streatham Park in south London, home to the Thrales

Thanks to his pension and to the hospitality of the Thrales, Johnson did not think he needed much extra money. He was not greedy. They thought that in return for this modest sum, so much less than the £4,500 that the Scots historian Robertson was offered for his *History of Charles V*, he would make a few judicious observations that could act as brief prefaces to the poems. What he gave them was a series of masterly accounts of 52 poets, in which he said something about the poets' lives before discussing their works. In the case of important authors, Johnson also plunged into elaborate analyses of their poetic character. What the publishers first printed, then, were short volumes with the accompanying essays. They rightly expected that Johnson's name would sell their books. What they could not have expected was that Johnson proved more attractive to read than the poems he introduced, so that his 'Essays' were printed separately.

Johnson wrote his *Prefaces*, whether long or short, off the top of his head. He had an aversion to research, so that he was at first angry with Boswell for arranging an interview for him the next day with Lord Marchmont, who had known Pope. *I shall not be in town tomorrow. I don't care to know about Pope*, he roared. *If it rained knowledge, I should hold out my hand; but I would not give myself the trouble to go in quest of it.*[180] A little later he said that if Lord Marchmont called on him, he would call on Lord Marchmont. Finally, when it was published, he had a copy of the first section of the *Lives* sent to Marchmont, Marchmont called on him and Johnson returned the visit and heard from Marchmont everything he had to say about Pope. He was thrilled at having had the interview and had the graciousness to admit to Boswell, *I would rather have given twenty pounds than not have come.*[181]

If it was hard to persuade him to gather first-hand evidence about the subject of the central life of the *Lives*, then it is easier to see that he did not add to his work when he thought that no work was needed. *The Life of Savage* written long ago, was inserted in the *Lives* and by its length alone suggested that a relatively minor poet was of major importance, whereas by 1780 Savage mattered, if at all, only to the few, like Johnson himself, who remembered him. As Goldsmith had written an account of Thomas Parnell, a friend of Pope's, Johnson felt under no obligation to add much of his own – and he took the opportunity to pay tribute to his own dead friend, *a man of such variety of powers and such felicity of performance, that he always seemed to do best what he was doing.*[182] Among Goldsmith's numerous accomplishments had been his poetry. As a poet, Goldsmith was better than most of those he had to write about, but there were said to be problems of copyright, so that only Johnson's encomium is there to indicate that one of two key poets of the mid-18th century had been omitted. The other was Johnson himself.

There is one even more famous personal passage, in the life of a forgotten poet, Edmund Smith. Mr Oldisworth had written an account of Smith that Johnson inserted without comment, and to which he added information gleaned from Gilbert Walmsley, *one of the first friends that literature procured me.*[183] This gave him an excuse to pay tribute to the benevolent Whig cleric, who had encouraged him in Lichfield when he was still in his late teens and in whose household he had met David Garrick, then only a mischievous schoolboy. But Garrick too was dead. *I am disappointed by that stroke of death*, he added, *which has eclipsed the gaiety of nations, and impoverished the public stock of humble pleasure.*[184] Garrick, seven years younger than Johnson, had died before him. That was why Johnson said he was *disappointed*, for he meant that Garrick's death was untimely as he himself expected to go first. He had been irritated by Garrick, jealous of Garrick, contemptuous of Garrick, yet he had never let anyone else criticise him in his presence, for only he knew and loved Garrick enough to see his failings. But Garrick had been kind to him, amusing and generous, and nobody had Garrick's ability to be at ease in any theatre or to command any audience, however grand. When David Garrick was buried in Westminster Abbey, close by the memorial to his idol Shakespeare, Johnson stood in silence, as tears fell down his cheeks.

It is the personal quality in Johnson's writing, even when he was writing about someone or something he did not know well, that makes his account of the poets so lively. Of Otway, who was valued for *Venice Preserved*, a play still performed, Johnson was embarrassed to report that he may have died from choking on a morsel of bread – his hunger made him all too anxious to devour anything – adding that he appeared to be a zealous royalist, and so *experienced what was in those days the common reward of loyalty – he lived and died neglected*.[185] And, even when tackling a figure such as James Thomson, the well-known author of *The Seasons*, Johnson did not mind exposing his own defects. Of *Liberty*, he wrote, *when it first appeared, I tried to read, and soon desisted. I have never tried again, and therefore will not hazard either praise or censure*.[186]

Johnson also had the gift of making his view of some of the poets only too clear. He dismissed the verses of John Sheffield, Duke of Buckinghamshire (1649–1720/21) as *often insipid*.[187] And when he wrote of a more considerable man, Matthew Prior, sometime ambassador at the court of Versailles, he indicated a familiar cause of writer's block: *in his private relaxation he revived the tavern*.[188] He added little details to enliven his narrative: Watts's father was a shoemaker, Collins's a hatter and Akenside's a butcher.[189] The information added nothing to a critical understanding of poetic ability, but it placed the men in their contexts.

Of John Phillips, the most revealing anecdote was that, *when he was at school, he seldom mingled in play with the other boys, but retired to his chamber, where his sovereign pleasure was to sit, hour after hour, while his hair was combed by somebody whose service he found means to procure*.[190] When he grew up, he kept the instincts of a solitary, for *I have been told that he was in company silent . . . and employed only upon the pleasures of his pipe*.[191] He was a clever man but not enough of a man to be a great writer. *What study could confer, Phillips had obtained* but he could not make up for defects in his character. *He seems not born to greatness and elevation*.[192]

Johnson himself had his eye set on the heights. His brief was to introduce the poets who had died between 1660 and 1775 in the order of death, and in his own mind he was clear who were the main ones. The most significant *Lives* are those of Abraham Cowley (1618–67), Milton, John Dryden, Joseph Addison, Alexander Pope and Jonathan Swift. Of these, the first two deal with poets who do not belong to his poetic world, for their literary assumptions were those of a previous age, while it was Dryden, Addison, Pope and Swift who had set standards for what is now called the Augustan style and which to Johnson was simply good modern writing.

Cowley is no longer a familiar author and, after Charles II came back to claim his throne in 1660, he was already approaching obsolescence. But he was the last representative of an important school of poetry that was rediscovered around 1914, the school whose master was John Donne. It was Johnson who gave this school the name we take for granted, for he named Cowley a 'Metaphysical' poet. By use of this term he meant to imply what to him was both a central issue and a curious one:

As Aristotle wrote *The Metaphysics* as a sequel to *The Physics* ('meta' means after), the title gave its name to the most abstruse part of philosophy, which deals with first principles. By applying the term 'metaphysical' to a group of poets, Johnson meant that they 'played' with images derived from profound ideas.

the predilection of 'Metaphysical' poets to seek their images from obscure branches of learning.

Cowley was educated at Westminster School and Cambridge, until he was ejected by the Puritans only took refuge in Oxford, while it was the royalist centre in the first civil war, and then in France, where he joined many royalist refugees and was secretary to Lord Jermyn.

Cowley was a precocious poet, whose early works were in print when he was just 13. In 1656, he was sent back to England to act as a sort of spy, but was quickly imprisoned and released only after the huge sum of £1,000 had been paid as a surety of his good behaviour. He then made his way back to Oxford, where many of the future founding fathers of the Royal Society were working. He became a Doctor of Medicine or 'physic' as it was then called and went into the country to study botany, as a principal part of medical treatment involved the use of herbs. When Charles II returned, Cowley expected some attractive post, but that did not materialise and, when he tried to write a play, it found no favour. In the end, he retired to Chertsey in Surrey and died there in 1667.

Evidently, Cowley was a learned man and the qualities in him that both fascinated and repelled Johnson came from his devotion to the cult of cleverness. Johnson thought it was a kind of writing that had been influenced immediately by that of Donne, *a man of very extensive and various knowledge*,[193] whom he thought Cowley's chief model. To illustrate his point, Johnson quoted extensively both from Cowley and from Donne. What he censured was the straining after effect, for Cowley seemed to lower grand conceptions by applying them without a sense of fitness. *The most splendid ideas drop their magnificence, if they are conveyed by words used commonly upon low and trivial occasions, debased by vulgar mouths and contaminated by inelegant applications.*[194]

If Cowley was the last representative of a school, Milton stood for nobody but himself. Johnson did not like him – he detested his republicanism, his hatred of obeying anyone else while demanding freedom for himself, his harsh treatment of his daughters – and he did not care for much that Milton had written. He acknowledged Milton's great gifts as a linguist, his wide reading in ancient and modern literature and his courage, but nothing would persuade him to care for any of the poems Milton published in 1645, except for two of the slighter works: 'L'Allegro' (the happy man) and 'Il Penseroso' (the melancholy man). Astutely, Johnson noted that Milton found it easier to be serious than to be light-hearted – and considering 'Comus' he stated that, for all its many imperfections, Milton anticipated his mature style. As a masque, a pageant-like entertainment that was popular at Charles I's court, 'Comus' was verbose, unactable and tedious, but feelings and words were often noble and it was a juvenile prelude to the epic on which Milton's reputation chiefly rests, *Paradise Lost*.

Like Milton, Johnson regarded epic as the grandest form of poetry and he saluted Milton for his ability to write at such a high level. And yet, much as he admired the poet's inventiveness and though he could see the point of his convoluted style, Johnson admitted that he could not wish the poem to be any longer. Milton *was born for whatever is arduous*[195] and Johnson believed that readers needed to relax.

It was this sense of the lure of moderation that made him love Addison. Today, Addison is not read as a poet except perhaps by those who have sung 'The spacious firmament on high', an ode that is considered a superb hymn both for its clarity of diction and because it gives voice to Newton's revolutionary vision of the universe, where the ancient idea of the music of the spheres has been hushed and heavenly orbits, ordered rationally, still move according to God's determining design: 'What though no real voice nor sound/ Amid the radiant orbs be found? . . . / The hand that made us is divine.'[196]

The ability to write prose that speaks rather than preaches was first devised by Dryden and, even if he had not written innumerable plays or thousands of lines of verse, he could still be admired for his ability to hint at conversations on literary topics with alert readers. What he learnt from writing for the theatre were the arts of declamation and deflation – prologues and epilogues written for actresses such as Nell Gwynn are delightful – but what spurred him to greatness was the crisis over the succession to the throne that ran from 1678 to 1681 and, again, in 1688. It all came down to one point: could England, a Protestant country, be ruled by a Catholic King?

During the first crisis, Dryden used his wit to ridicule the attempt by the Whigs to substitute the oldest of Charles II's bastards, the Duke of Monmouth, for the legitimate heir, Charles's brother James. And in 'Absalom and Achitophel', he wrote the funniest political satire of the century.

When James became King, Dryden identified himself with the royal cause to such a degree that he became a Catholic. Johnson was not sure how sincere he was, but in the end gave him the benefit of the doubt (Dryden did raise his sons as Catholics). Regardless, it did not stop him from laughing at a passage in 'The Hind and the Panther', an allegory in which the first beast is the Catholic church and the second the Anglican church. Johnson was not impressed by the ability of animals to discuss the Christian creed.

By a strange coincidence, Dryden's principal poetic heir, Pope, was also a Catholic. An only child of elderly parents, always well-to-do even though Catholics were liable to double taxation, as a child Pope was crippled by a disease that left him a tiny hunchback, possibly impotent and always in pain. Encouraged as a child by aged men of letters, he soon decided to devote himself exclusively to poetry.

A man with shrewd business instincts, he translated Homer (with some help), partly because Dryden had translated Virgil, partly because it gave him a secure income that helped him buy a villa in Twickenham – Catholics were forbidden to own property in London – where he could concentrate on gardening as well as writing. Early poems, of which the most familiar is 'The Rape of the Lock', struck a light tone but in the late 1720s, he began a

A lithograph of Alexander Pope from the portrait by Hudson

general war on dullness – the dull were personal enemies or just writers not as good as him – and this earned him a reputation as waspish and disdainful.

At one stage, Johnson rounded on Pope for thinking that only he and his friends were people with sound moral and aesthetic values. Of all the recent poets, he found Pope the most gifted but he charged him with seeming to believe that *to want money is to want everything*.[197] Pope, alas, was a snob.

It was Johnson's veneration for naturalness that explained some of his critical stances. Of the Restoration dramatists, Congreve was regarded as the supreme master of sparkling dialogue, but to Johnson it was a grave failing that *the contest of smartness is never intermitted*[198] and that his characters had *very little of nature*.[199] Johnson found that much of Thomas Gray also suffered from artificiality and was relieved that in the *Elegy in a Country Churchyard* he could concur with the views of the common reader.

In spite of respecting *the common reader*,[200] he seemed vindictive in his refusal to allow much merit in Swift. *Gulliver's Travels* has endured as a popular classic, and Swift's prose can seem more modern than much of Johnson's, as some passages can be enjoyed by children. Johnson acknowledged the book's success but added that *no rules of judgement were applied to a book written in open defiance of truth and regularity*.[201] Even Boswell wondered why Johnson was so harsh on Swift.

Johnson had not set out to flatter his readers, but he also did not condescend to them either. Above all, he kept in mind the object he had set himself: to be accessible. Today, only scholars of the 18th century continue to read many of the works he discussed. Since he wrote, the Victorians popularised the Romantic revolution started by William Wordsworth (1770–1850) and Samuel Taylor Coleridge (1772–1834), and the shock of the first world war began a process of freeing poets from a singing voice that was no longer natural.

No critic in the early 21st century can write with the assurance of Johnson and no one else has ever been so fascinating a guide to over a hundred years of poetry. Among English literary histories, Johnson's *Lives* has no equal.

Having completed his final masterpiece, Johnson might have expected to live out his days in comfort, poised at the centre of London literary life, caring for his household of eccentrics, basking in the comforts of Streatham Park. But if he had hoped for tranquillity, it was denied him.

There were some compensations in public life. If the news of the war in America became progressively worse and if Britain managed to find itself at loggerheads with every other European naval power, then one of Johnson's political ideals seemed close to fulfilment. He had spoken out against encouraging the mob, and after 1780 he seemed to be vindicated. In that year, a half-mad Scots nobleman, Lord George Gordon (1751–93), called for a Protestant protest against the slight mitigation of anti-Catholic laws that made it easier for Catholics to practise their religion privately in the capital.

What followed was a week of looting and destruction, during which the authorities lost control of London. Johnson wrote a brief account of what happened. He noted that no less a person than John Wilkes had helped to repress the rioters and this was a necessary prelude to one of Boswell's cleverest plans: setting up meetings between his mentor and the political figure whom Johnson had most detested. Wilkes could be charming and Johnson was willing to be won over. In the end, the two thoroughly enjoyed their conversations.

Johnson always had a weakness for men of charm, and in March 1780 he was devastated by the loss of Topham Beauclerk. He wrote to remind Boswell: *His wit and his folly, his acuteness and his maliciousness, his merriment and reasoning are now over.*[202] As his friend lay dying, Johnson had cried out, *I would walk to the extent of the diameter of the earth to save him*.[203]

Worse was to follow. In September, Henry Thrale had another election to fight in Southwark. As usual, Johnson was at hand to help but the government was unpopular and Thrale was a sick man. He had caused himself financial trouble by trying to beat Whitbread in terms of the quantity of beer he brewed. He ate immoderately and he took little exercise. And he lost his parliamentary seat.

In the autumn of 1779, he had had the first of a series of strokes. Hester suggested a stay in Brighton and a move to Grosvenor Square and there, Johnson would have a room, too. But on 3 April 1781, after an enormous meal, Thrale became mortally ill. While Hester took to her room in panic, Johnson sat up all night with his old friend and at five o'clock in the morning he felt the last flicker of his pulse.

The death of Thrale led to the unravelling of Johnson's private life. Some wags thought he should marry Hester; she was anxious to start life anew. She quickly sold off the brewery – there was no male heir to run it – and she began to look for romance. She was a young widow, lively and attractive, whose life had been restricted by life in the nursery and by commercial concerns. She had married out of necessity; she concluded that this time she owed it to herself to marry for love.

In the end, she chose Gabriele Piozzi, her children's music teacher, an Italian and a Catholic. If she went ahead with the marriage, she would not want Johnson as a permanent resident in her house. Still, they corresponded for over a year. Johnson did not see Hester and then, abruptly on 30 June 1783, Hester wrote to him to tell him her plans. She would marry Piozzi, whatever her daughters, whatever anybody else thought. Johnson was appalled at her choice. He thought she was forfeiting her children, her fame and her faith (he could not know that Piozzi would die an Anglican). Later he wrote more temperately but the damage had been done. Both of them had hurt each other too much and, however much they tried to resuscitate it, their friendship was dead.

Half her life lay in front of Hester. Eventually she left the city where she had never quite felt at home, and ten years later she built herself a fine house, Brynbella, near her beloved Welsh mountains. Johnson stayed on in London, which was the world to him, though there were excursions: he kept up with his Lichfield friends, especially his step-daughter, Lucy Porter; he went to Oxford and he went to Birmingham.

He had lost another friend, when his breakfast companion, Dr Levet, died and he had an elegy printed in the *Gentleman's Magazine*, on which he had worked so long ago with Cave: 'Condemned to hope's delusive mine,/ As on we toil from day to day./ By sudden blasts, or slow decline,/ Our social comforts drop away. . .'[204]

That slow decline he now experienced himself. He found it difficult to breathe – he suffered from asthma – and he endured that standard 18th-century complaint known as dropsy, a feeling of swelling that could be a symptom of many diseases and a surgeon lanced his swollen legs to let out the water. Old and new friends who knew of his condition came to visit him.

Religion, which had so often distressed him, seemed to give him some serenity. He dictated a will leaving individuals with some memento they would like, so that the scholarly Bennet

Drawing of Johnson on his deathbed

Langton received his polyglot or multilingual Bible, Reynolds got his French dictionary and his own copy of the *Dictionary*, and the bulk of his estate went to, Frank Barber.

On 13 December, he died. A week later, he was buried in Westminster Abbey, in the presence of members of the Literary Club who were in town, including Burke, Banks and Langton.

After his death there was a rush to publish memoirs. Sir John Hawkins had known him longest and was quick to make himself known but, as Johnson's literary friends found him unclubable, so too the public found him uninteresting.

Two writers had a stronger claim for attention. Hester Piozzi (previously Thrale) was keen that her side of the story should be heard but though her *Anecdotes of Doctor Johnson* are full of material that only she could have provided, her impartiality was always suspect, because she was always on her guard.

Boswell, however, was more cunning. As a foretaste, he published his *Journal of a Tour to the Hebrides* first, so that when his *Life* came out, dedicated to Reynolds and replete with documents, he had already created an appetite for his main course. It quickly became obvious that here was a work of genius worthy of its subject, the most complete account of any English person that had ever been made. Johnson was not just the supreme man of letters of his age; he encapsulated that age, so that it quickly became the age of Johnson. As a person, he was an archetype.

Today, Johnson does not so easily occupy the centre of attention. Many of his writings have dated, partly because his language is more Latinate than modern English. The England – as well as the English language that he knew – has vanished. He assumed that the final arbiter of government was the King, he took it for granted that few men and no women had the right to vote, he defended the privileged position of the Church of England. His view of English literature seems too narrowly based on knowledge of the classical tradition. But in his humane attitudes towards blacks, towards the poor and the defeated, he displayed a sympathy that raises him above the prejudices of his class and time. As an adult, he lived through three major wars without becoming bellicose. He never made the mistake of thinking works of art more important than the lives that shape the art. Yet it is fitting that his body lies close to Garrick's, in the Poets' Corner of Westminster Abbey.

Notes

The guiding principal for researching this book has been to refer to the most readily accessible texts. A good university library will contain the editions that a serious student will need, but someone with less rigorous designs on Johnson will want texts available in bookshops, on the internet or in a public library.

The books referred to most frequently are abbreviated as follows:

MW: *Samuel Johnson, The Major Works*, ed Donald Greene (Oxford, 2000).
D: *Dictionary of the English Language* (1755) reproduced by Time Books (1979), in which entries appear alphabetically but without any system of page numbering.
PP: Samuel Johnson, *Prose and Poetry*, edited by Mona Wilson (Rupert Hart Davis, 1966). I have taken comments on individual plays by Shakespeare from this anthology.
LP: *The Lives of the Poets*, Everyman Library edition (J.M. Dent & Sons Ltd., 1964).
SE: *Samuel Johnson: Selected Essays*, ed David Womersley (Penguin: London, 2003).
PW: *The Political Writings of Dr Johnson*, ed John Hardy (Routledge and Kegan Paul: London, 1968).
JB: *A Journey to the Western Islands* and Boswell's *The Journal of a Tour to the Hebrides*, ed Peter Levi (Penguin, 1984). These two works are usually coupled together, as in this case.
B: James Boswell, *Life of Johnson*, World's Classic edition (Oxford, 1998).
Among modern biographers, I rely chiefly on three. Quotations from the works of two 18th-century Johnsonians, Sir John Hawkins and Mrs Thrale, have been taken from these books.
C/Young: James L. Clifford, *Young Samuel Johnson* (Heinemann, 1955).
C/Dictionary: James L Clifford, *Dictionary Johnson* (Heinemann, 1980).
C/Hester: James L Clifford, *Hester Lynch Piozzi* (Oxford, 1987).
WJB: Walter Jackson Bate, *Samuel Johnson* (Chatto & Windus, 1978).
JW: John Wain, *Samuel Johnson* (Macmillan, 1974).

1 James L. Clifford, *Young Samuel Johnson* (Heinemann, 1955), p. 6.
2 C/Young, p.18f
3 C/Young, p.19
4 Walter Jackson Bate, *Samuel Johnson* (Chatto & Windus, 1978), p. 19
5 WJB, p. 22
6 Mrs Thrale, quoted in C/Young, p. 23
7 C/Young, p.45

8 James Boswell, *Life of Johnson* (Oxford, 1998), p. 34

9 C/Young, p.55

10 WJB, p 50

11 *The Lives of the Poets* (J M Dent & Sons Ltd., 1964) vol. I, p.294

12 C/Young, p. 106

13 C/Young, p.118

14 B, pp. 50–51

15 B, p.76

16 *Samuel Johnson, The Major Works*, ed by Donald Greene (Oxford, 2000), p.6

17 Jonathan Swift, *Gulliver's Travels* I, 3

18 C/Young, p. 243

19 W, p 56

20 W, p 58

21 W, p 67

22 Alexander Pope, *The Rape of the Lock*, canto III, lines 7–8

23 Quoted by Richard Holmes, *Dr Johnson and Mr Savage*, p.99

24 Words by James Thomson, *The Masque of Alfred*, music by Dr Arne

25 Quoted by Richard Holmes, *Dr J and Mrs*, p.44

26 LPII, p.142

27 *The Lives of the Poets* (J M Dent & Son Ltd., 1964) vol.II, p.142

28 W, p.319–20

29 *A Dictionary of the English Language*

30 W, p.312

31 W, p.135

32 LPII, p. 261

33 D

34 D

35 W, p.328

36 D

37 D

38 D

39 D

40 D

41 D

42 W, p.782

43 W, p.12

44 Juvenal, *Satire X*, line 356

45 Juvenal, *Satire X*, line 81

46 W, p.15

47 W, p.17

48 W, p.12

49 W, p.21

50 B, p.281

51 B, p.312

52 B, p.175

53 B, p.176

54 B, p.173

55 B, p.173

56 B, p. 615

57 John Hardy, *The Political Writings of Dr Johnson* (Routledge and Kegan Paul, 1968), pp. 16–17

58 PW, p. 25

59 PW, p. 33

60 PW, pp. 33–34

61 PW, p. 38

62 W, p. 547

63 *The Idler* 11 contains this reference to slavery. I have been unable to find this essay in one of the most accessible anthologies, so I must refer the reader to the Yale edition of *The Idler and The Adventurer* (London and New York, 1963). This is curious, as the essay begins with one of Johnson's most famous remarks: *It is commonly observed, that when two Englishmen meet, their first talk is of the weather.*

64 David Womersley, *Samuel Johnson: Selected Essays* (Penguin, 2003), p. 422

65 'The Idler' 10 mocks the political prejudices of Tom Tempest and Jack Sneaker. . . David Womersley, *Samuel Johnson: Selected Essays* (Penguin, 2003), pp. 413–414

66 'The Idler' 60 and 61 mock Dick Minim's literary career . . . SE, pp. 464–471

67 Basil Willey, *The eighteenth century background: studies on the idea of nature in the thought of the period*. (Harmondsworth Penguin, 1972) has a chapter, Cosmic Toryism, on Alexander Pope's 'Essay on Man' and Soames Jenyns.

68 Alexander Pope, 'Essay on Man', Epistle I, lines 293–94

69 W, p. 523

70 W, p. 527

71 W, p. 527

72 W, p. 534

73 W, p. 535

74 W, p. 536

75 W, p. 542

76 James L Clifford, *Dictionary Johnson* (Heinemann, 1980), p. 183

77 W, p.784

78 W, p.784

79 B, p. 241–42

80 W, p.418

81 W, p.418

82 W, p.418

83 W, p.377

84 W, p.355

85 D

86 D

87 B, p. 265

88 Charles Churchill, *The Ghost* . . . [[See above]] C/Dictionary, pp. 259–260

89 Charles Churchill, *The Ghost* . . . B, p.227

90 North Briton, XII . . . [[See above] C/Dictionary, p. 271

91 B, p.296

92   This passage from Johnson's *Prayers and Meditations* is mentioned in B, p. 254

93   C/Dictionary, p. 281

94   C/Dictionary, p. 281

95   C/Dictionary, p. 293

96   B, p.1261

97   B, p.277

98   B, p. 327

99   B, p. 444

100 B, p. 214

101 B, p. 494

102 B, p. 415

103 B, p. 416

104 B, p. 662

105 James L Clifford, *Hester Lynch Piozzi* (Oxford, 1987), p. 55

106 C/Hester, p. 56

107 Strictly, the words apply to Mrs Thrale after her husband's death. As an executor of Thrale's will and, thus, involved in the sale of the Thrale brewery, Johnson remarked: *We are not here to sell a parcel of boilers and vats, but the potentiality of growing rich, beyond the dreams of avarice.* Thrale had been the wealthy person: now it was his widow. B, p. 1132

107 B, p.416

108 W, p.441

109 PP, p. 631

110 PP, p. 615

111 PP, p. 531

112 W, p. 322

113 W, p. 438

114 PP, p. 546

115 W, p. 584

116 PP, p.609

117 PP, p.609

118 W, p.432

119 PP, p. 593

120 *a stupid slut* – the context indicates that what exasperated him was her lack of decisiveness. WJB, p. 503

121 WJB, p. 407

122 WJB, p. 500–1

123 WJB, p. 268

124 John Wain, *Samuel Johnson*, p. 268.

125 C/Hester, p. 60

126 PW, p.40

127 PW, p.40

128 PW, p.40

129 PW, p.42

130 *The False Alarm*, PW, p.43

131 *The False Alarm*, PW, p.59

132 PW, p.61

133 PW, p. 62

134 PW, p.67

135 PW, p. 76

136 PW, p. 76

137 B, p. 450

138 Reynolds, quoted in Ian McIntyre, *Joshua Reynolds*, p.193

139 Johnson, quoted in Ian McIntyre, *Joshua Reynolds*, p.193

140 Mrs Thrale, *Anecdotes of Dr Johnson*, quoted by Walter Jackson Bate, *Samuel Johnso*n, p. 426

141 B, p. 396

142 WJB, p. 424

143 B, p. 421

144 B, p. 537

145 B, p. 859

146 B, p. 722

147 WJB, p. 466

148 B, p. 723

149 B, p.302

150 JB, p.50

151 JB, p.51

152 JB, p.51

153 JB, p.54

154 JB, p.58

155 JB, p.58

156 JB, p.61

157 JB, p.242

158 JB, p.254

159 JB, p.265

160 JB, p. 80

161 JB, p.277

162 JB, p.363

163 JB, p.331

164 JB, p.361

165 JB, pp. 140–41

166 *Having passed my time almost wholly in cities, I may have been surprised by modes of life and appearance of nature, that are familiar to men of wider survey and more varied conversation. Novelty and ignorance must always be reciprocal, and I cannot but be conscious that my thoughts on national manners, are the thoughts of one who has seen but little. Johnson, A Journey to the Western Islands of Scotland*, p. 152.
Johnson's 18th-century English may confuse the modern reader. *The Dictionary* can help. Survey is defined as *view* or *prospect*, so that *men of wider survey* are people who have seen more. *Conversation*: Johnson derives from the Latin word conversation, which does not always mean an activity concerned with talk (meanings 1 and 2). Johnson's meaning 3 is *Commerce, intercourse, familiarity* – here *commerce* does not involve trade, *intercourse* does not involve sex, so familiarity is the most useful definition.

167 B, p. 642

168 B, pp. 643–4
169 PW, p. 92
170 PW, p. 96
171 PW, p. 113
172 PW, p. 132
173 B, p. 828
174 B, p. 831
175 B, p. 834
176 B, p. 834
177 B, p. 835
178 'When I survey the wondrous cross' first appeared in *Hymns and spiritual songs*
(1707), 'Our (now usually 'Oh') God, our help in ages past in The Psalms of
David' (1719). Both hymns are accessible in virtually any modern hymnal of
any Christian church.
179 B, pp. 988–89
180 B, p. 1024
181 LPI, p. 311
182 LPI, p. 294
183 LPI, p. 295
184 LPI, p. 295
185 LPI, p. 144
186 LPI, p. 292
187 LPI, p. 378
188 LPI, p. 395
189 LPII, pp. 293, 313, 371
190 LPI, p. 273
191 LPI, p. 275
192 LPI, p. 277
193 LPI, p. 13
194 LPI, p. 39
195 LPI, p. 114
196 ...*What though no real* ... *The hand that made us is divine* The words come
from an ode, 'The spacious firmament on high', published by Joseph Addison
in *The Spectator* of 20 August, 1712, after an essay on the right way to
strengthen and confirm faith in the mind of man. The ode has become a
famous hymn and is sometimes sung to a tune by Haydn.
197 LPII, p. 205
198 LPII, p. 8
199 LPII, p. 8
200 LPII, p. 392
201 LPII, p. 261
202 B, p. 1047
203 B, p. 1072
204 W, p. 35

Chronology

Year	Age	Life
1709		7 September: Birth of Samuel Johnson in Lichfield, Staffordshire. Taken to London to be touched by Queen Anne for scrufola.
1717	7	Enters Lichfield Grammar School.
1728–29	19–20	At Pembroke College, Oxford.
1731	22	Death of Michael Johnson (father).
1735	26	Marries Elizabeth Porter.

Chronology

Year	History	Culture
1709	First Russian prisoners sent to Siberia. In Russia, the Great Plague. Rising of Afghans at Kandahar under Mir Vais. Battle of Poltava: Swedish hegemony in the Baltic ends.	Bartolomeo Cristofori builds the first pianoforte. William Byrd, *The Secret Diary of W B Westover*.
1717	In North America, Shenandoah Valley settled by Europeans; native Indians evicted.	Handel, *Water Music*. Antoine Watteau, *Embarkation for the Isle of Cytheria*.
1728–29	Vitus Bering discovers straits which separate northeast Asia from northwest America (Bering Straits). North and South Carolina become British colonies. In China, Emperor Yung Cheng prohibits opium smoking. Stephen Gray discovers that some bodies conduct electricity.	John Gay, *The Beggars' Opera*. Alexander Pope, *The Dunciad*. Swift, A Modest Proposal. James and Benjamin Franklin, *The Pennsylvania Gazette*. In Constantinople, publication of secular Turkish works begins.
1731	Grand duke of Tuscany (last of the Medicis) recognises Don Carlos as his heir.	Pierre Carlet de Chamblain de Marivaux, *La Vie de Marianne*. Hogarth, *Harlot's Progress*.
1735	In China, Chien Lung becomes emperor.	Rameau, *Les Indes galantes*. Hogarth, *Rake's Progress*.

Year	Age	Life
1736	27	Opens school at Edial.
1737	28	Death of Nathanial Johnson (brother). Leaves for London.
1738	29	Publishes 'London'.
1746	37	Signs contract for *the Dictionary*.
1749	40	Publishes 'Vanity of Human Wishes'. Publishes and acts in production of Irene.
1750–52	41–43	Publishes *The Rambler*.
1752	43	Death of Elizabeth Johnson (wife).
1753–54	44–45	Publishes articles in *The Adventurer*.

Year	History	Culture
1736	In Edinburgh, Porteous riots. In Britain, statutes against witchcraft are repealed. Pope Clement XII condemns freemasonry.	Giovanni Battista Pergolesi, *Stabat Mater*. French Academy sponsors an expedition to Lapland to measure the arc of meridian.
1737	In North America, William Byrd founds Richmond, Virginia.	Chardin, *The Draughtsman*.
1738	In Britain, John Wesley begins Methodist revival.	Handel, *Israel in Egypt* and *Saul*. In St Petersburg, Imperial Ballet School founded.
1746	In Spain, Philip V dies; Ferdinand VI becomes king. In Scotland, Battle of Culloden: final defeat of Jacobites.	Etiénne Bonnot and Abbé Condillac, *Essai sur l'origine des connaissances humaines*. Albert von Haller, *Disputationes Anatomicae Selectiones*.
1749	Halifax, Nova Scotia, is established as a fortress. First settlement of the Ohio Co.	J S Bach, *Die Kunst der Fuge*. Henry Fielding, *The History of Tom Jones, A Foundling*.
1750–52	In Europe, tea becomes fashionable drink. Britain adopts Gregorian Calendar.	In 1750, the English Jockey Club is founded. In 1750, In 1750, 'Capability' Brown finishes Croom Court Gardens in 1751.
1752	In Britain, Murder Act lays down that murderers are not to receive burials.	Gluck completes his opera *La Clemenz de Tito*.
1753–54	France faces bankruptcy. Louis XV exiles the Paris parliament, only to recall it the next year.	Samuel Richardson, *Sir Charles Grandison*, vols. 1–4.

Year	Age	Life
1754	45	Publishes *Dictionary of the English Language*. Granted honorary MA by Oxford.
1758–60	49–51	Writes 'The Idler' column in *The Universal Chronicle*.
1759	50	Death of Sarah Johnson (mother).
1762	53	Awarded pension of £300 per year.
1763	54	Meets James Boswell.
1764	55	Literary Club formed.
1765	56	Publishes edition of Shakespeare. Meets Henry and Hester Thrale.
1766	57	Helps Robert Chambers with Vinerian Lectures. Suffers severe depression.

Year	History	Culture
1754	Anglo-French war breaks out in North America.	Hogarth, *The Election.* Chippendale, *The Gentleman and Cabinetmaker's Directory.*
1758–60	John Forbes and George Washington take Fort Duquesne, subsequently renamed Pittsburg.	John and Robert Adam finish Harewood House. The silk hat is invented in Florence in 1760.
1759	British victory in Quebec; Royal Navy defeats French at Quiberon Bay.	Voltaire, *Candide.* British Museum opened.
1762	Tsarina Elizabeth dies, succeeded by Peter III, who is assassinated six months later and succeeded by Catherine II.	W A Mozart and his sister (aged six and ten) begin touring Europe giving concerts. Goldoni, *Le Baruffe chiozzotte.*
1763	Peace of Paris between Britain, France and Spain ends Seven Years' War; Britain secures Canada, Nova Scotia, Cape Breton, St Vincent, Tobago, Dominica, Grenada, Senegal and Minorca from France, and Florida from Spain.	Hume, *History of Great Britain.* Kant publishes moral proof of God's existence. Karl Philip Emanuel Bach, *Sonata for Piano.*
1764	John Wilkes expelled from Commons having written seditious libel; riots in London in favour of Wilkes.	J J Winckelmann, *History of Ancient Art.* Voltaire, *Philosophical Dictionary.* Robert Adam, Kenwood House, Middlesex.
1765	Joseph II of Austria becomes Holy Roman Emperor.	Horace Walpole's *The Castle of Otranto* founds the English romantic school of fiction.
1766	British Parliament passes Act declaring Britain's right to tax the American colonies.	Helps Robert Chambers with Vinerian Lectures. Suffers severe depression.

Year	Age	Life
1770	61	Publishes *The False Alarm*.
1771	62	Publishes *Thoughts on the Late Transactions respecting Falkland's Islands*.
1773	64	With Boswell, tours Scotland.
1774	65	With the Thrales, tours Wales. Publishes *The Patriot*.
1775	66	Publishes *Journey to the Western Islands of Scotland*. Publishes *Taxation no tyranny*. Awarded honorary doctorate by Oxford. With the Thrales, tours France.
1777	68	Unsuccessful campaign to gain a pardon for Dr Dodd.
1779–81	70–72	Publishes *The Lives of the Poets*. Henry Thrale dies in 1781.
1784	75	13 December: Dies. 20 December: Buried in the Poets' Corner, Westminster Abbey.

Year	History	Culture
1770	Boston Massacre. French Dauphin marries Marie Antoinette.	Edmund Burke, *Thoughts on Present Discontents*.
1771	Maupeou overthrow the French Parlements. Russia completes conquest of the Crimea.	Publishes *Thoughts on the Late Transactions respecting Falkland's Islands*.
1773	Boston Tea Party.	
1774	Louis XVI becomes king. British parliament passes Coercive Acts against Boston and Massachusetts.	Goethe, *The Sorrows of Young Werther*. C W Gluck, *Iphigénie en Aulide*.
1775	War of American Independence opens with defeat of British at Lexington and Concord. George Washington appointed commander-in-chief. British victory at Bunker Hill.	Goethe accepts appointment at ducal court of Weimar. P A C Beaumarchais' *Barber of Seville* produced in Paris after two years' prohibition. R B Sheridan, *The Rivals*.
1777	Congress adopts Confederation Articles of perpetual union of United States of America (first US constitution).	J Haydn, *La Roxolane* Symphony. C W Gluck, *Armide*.
1779–81	Spain declares war on Britain. Gordon riots in London. Maria Theresa of Austria dies. End of the American revolution.	Canova, *Daedalus and Icarus*. James Gillray's earliest satirical cartoon. In 1779 the Derby is first run on Epsom Racecourse.
1784	Treaty of Constantinople: Russia annexes Crimea.	J G Herder, *Ideas towards a Philosophy of History*.

Further Reading

PRIMARY WORKS

The chief biographies of Samuel Johnson are: James Boswell, *Journal of a Tour to the Hebrides with Samuel Johnson*, LLD. (1785); Hester Thrale Piozzi, *Anecdotes of Samuel Johnson*, LLD. (1786); Sir John Hawkins, *The Life of Samuel Johnson*, LLD. (1787); and James Boswell, *The Life of Samuel Johnson*, LLD. (1791). Of these, the Anecdotes are readable, Boswell's two works are superb and the *Life* has been reprinted many times. The most accessible edition of Boswell's and Johnson's two accounts of their travels in Scotland is that by Peter Levi (Penguin, 1984).

The Yale edition of the works of Samuel Johnson aims to print everything written by Johnson. In 2004, the edition reaches volume xvii. The final volume will be no. xxiv.

Johnson aimed to write for the common reader and, as an author, he is much better read in extracts. There are numerous editions of his works: of his Poems, such as that by J D Fleeman (Penguin and Yale, 1971); of *Rasselas*, such as that by John Hardy (Oxford, 1988); of a selection of his essays by David Womersley (Penguin, 2003), of *The Lives of the Poets* (J M Dent, 1964). There is an edition of *The Life of Richard Savage* by Clarence Tracy (Oxford, 1971).

Johnson's political writings are published by John Hardy (London, 1968). The Dictionary, in its first and fourth editions, is available on a Cambridge CD-Rom, and has been reproduced in facsimile reprints (1967, 1968, 1979, 1980). His *Letters* have been edited in five volumes (Princeton and Oxford, 1992–94). Selections of his works have been edited by Mona Wilson (Rupert Hart David, 1966), Bertrand H Bronson (Rhinehart, 1971) and Donald Greene (Oxford, 1984).

SECONDARY WORKS

The best modern biographies of Samuel Johnson are: the two careful books by James L Clifford, *Young Sam Johnson* (New York, 1955) and *Dictionary Johnson* (New York, 1979); *Samuel Johnson*, the monumental account by Walter Jackson Bate (New York and London, 1977); and *Samuel Johnson: a biography*, by John Wain (London, 1974), the most attractive work for anyone setting out to understand Johnson.

In recent years, two books have made subtle additions to the understanding of the great man: *Dr Johnson and Mr Savage* by Richard Holmes (HarperCollins, 1993); and *Boswell's Presumptuous Task* by Adam Sisman (Hamish Hamilton, 2000).

Of Johnson's friends, several have been well served. Among studies of Hester Thrale, the biography by James L Clifford, *Hester Lynch Piozzi* (Mrs Thrale) (Oxford, 1987) is one of the most judicious. Beryl Bainbridge's novel, *According to Queeney* (London, 2002) tries to get inside the mind of an awkward observer, Mrs Thrale's oldest daughter. Ian MacIntyre has turned his attention successively to *Garrick* (Allen Lane, 1999) and to *Joshua Reynolds* (Allen Lane, 2003). F.P. Lock has written the first part of a life of *Edmund Burke* (Oxford, 1998), which covers the years 1730–1784, so ending in the year of Johnson's death. Carola Hicks, *Improper Pursuits* (St Martin's Press, 2002), focusses on the adventurous life of Lady Di Beauclerck, but is also the liveliest account available of her husband Topham.

There is an attractive evocation of *Dr Johnson's London* by Liza

Picard (*Weidenfeld & Nicolson*, 2000). And on the social life of England in the 18th century or almost anything related to the period, there is no more lively writer than the late Roy Porter, as in *English society in the eighteenth century* (Penguin, 1990) or in his discussions of the history of London, enlightenment, medicine or madness.

Lawrence Lipking has written on *The Ordering of the Arts in Eighteenth Century England* (Princeton, 1970) and discusses Reynolds, Sir John Hawkins and Charles Burney as well as Johnson. Jean H Hagstrum has analysed *Johnson's Literary Criticism* (Chicago, 1967) and James T Boulton has produced evidence of the way in which Johnson himself has been read in Johnson: *The Critical Heritage* (London, 1971).

Of all introductions to the academic study of Johnson the most useful aid is Greg Clingham's edition of *The Cambridge Companion to Samuel Johnson* (Cambridge, 1997), but the reader should be cautious. Johnson did not set up the Johnson industry. He meant to be read by the common reader and the common reader does not usually study for a doctorate in English literature. There is no substitute for dipping into Boswell and into some of Johnson's own more accessible works.

Picture Sources

The author and publishers wish to express their thanks to the following sources of illustrative material and/or permission to reproduce it. They will make proper acknowledgements in future editions in the event that any omissions have occurred.

Getty Images: pp. 43, 46, 53, 78. Mary Evans Picture Library: pp. i, iii, 5, 32, 38, 51, 58, 67, 106, 112, 135. Topham Picturepoint: pp. 12, 16, 20, 21, 23, 29, 56, 70, 74, 82, 84, 92, 94, 100, 121, 123, 131.

Index